Options Trading Crash Course

The ultimate guide to investing and making money with options trading

Marlon Diggory

Table of contents

Chapter 1: Introduction

What Are Options?

Since the 1970s, options markets have been running in many countries across major stock exchanges. Since then, in most situations, these markets have experienced significant increases in both the number of trading options and the variety of available options. Why? Since options are an incredible tool for trading that can be used in a wide range of strategies. Options strategies can differ in time frame, risk, and intent to satisfy a wide range of investors and trader's needs. We'll describe what options are in, how they operate, and some of the other ways they can be used to improve your trading returns.

We will refer to exchange-traded options over stocks or shares. These are options that can be bought and exchanged through a regulated market such as the Australian Securities Market (ASX) and are the option category most widely traded. This enables us to simplify the discussion by introducing the different options components and attributes.

There are also opportunities for listed hedge funds (ETFs), indexes and currencies. There are also options provided by businesses that have varying terms and conditions from the options exchanged in return.

We describe an option as a contract giving one an opportunity to buy or sell a given asset at a stated price (commonly called the strike) until the expiration date. Options contracts indirectly own a section of the company but allows for a right of buying or selling a lot (considered to be 100 shares) of the shares of the company. If you exercise a call option, stipulated as a right to buy shares, you will then own shares. If not, you have the derivative products that derive value from stocks. When you buy an option contract typically you will pay a predetermined premium to have the right to purchase or sell the stock. The further the expiration date is away for the current date, the premium charge becomes more. Likewise, if you have the choice, the option value will decay/deteriorate over the period at an exponential rate, closer you are to the expiration date. The term "naked" refers sell selection option when one doesn't have the underlying assets or have some cash set to shield such a choice, the contract should be implemented. Purchase options can only be done in many representing 100 shares. Option contract only allows for the right to buy or sell shares, but not directly invest in stocks. Only option contracts remain good until the expiration date. Derivatives are kind effects that derive/develop their value from an underlying asset, such as commodities, stocks, or currencies. Options gave the purchaser the opportunity (not obligation) of selling (through selection of a put) or buying (via call options) securities or financial assets at a defined price (the strike price) for a certain period. It is utilized to hedge market risks that are related to asset prices.

As we have seen, options are the right to buy an asset at a certain price on or before a specific date.

For instance, if you have an interest in purchasing a new boat, but you were not completely sure you were ready to pay for it, but you didn't want the price of the boat to change. Let's say it is May 1st. You could buy the OPTION to buy the boat on June 15th for the price the boat is currently right now. Assuming the boat is $50,000 you could pay $ 2,500 for the right to buy the boat on June 15th for $ 50,000. Now a couple things could arise out of this situation. At the end of May you find out the boat was secretly made of gold, so its value sky rockets to $500,000. Well lucky for you, you still have to option to buy the bought for $50,000 before June 15! Your total profit would be 500,000- 52,000 for a total of 448,000 dollars! Another situation could arise where at the end of May you find out the boat's wood is rotting. Unfortunately for you, the boats value plummets to $ 10,000. Now your option to buy the boat at $ 50,000 is worthless and you should just let it expire.

The last hypothetical situation with your boat option is that you put yourself in a coma to become a pro lucid dreamer, and you are so out of it you don't wake up until July 4th! Now this really sucks because you only had until June 15th to buy your boat at $ 50,000. Now your option is worthless.

What Are Stocks?

A stock is a kind of securities. The stock we usually refer to refers to common stock, which is a share of ordinary rights in the company's management and that closely deals with the profit and distribution of property. Conceptually, stocks are stock certificates issued by a company limited by shares to investors when raising capital, representing the ownership of the company by its holders (i.e. shareholders).

Share is a fractional ownership of a company. Own a company's stock means that you own part of the company proportional to the number of shares the company has outstanding. For example, if you possess 50 shares of a firm that has a total of 1,000 shares, you have 5% of the company. Shares come with all existing tenures with capital assets. However, shareholders are listed in the line of creditors when a company files for bankruptcy. It should be noted that when you buy shares, you receive dividends paid to shareholders. However, when you short stocks, you will be responsible for the payment of such dividends. When you buy stocks, you can buy any quantity you want from the stock as long as someone is willing to sell that amount. Stocks provide direct investment into the company through partial ownership. When you buy or short stocks, your position remains open until you sell or close your short. To benefit from the decline in stock prices, traders can short of financial instruments, which typically generate unlimited losses and margin if the share price rises again, you can only short stocks with the margin trading enabled accounts.

Who Is a Broker?

Most options accounts are set up separately to a share trading account.

In order to set up an options account, you will

need to fill out some paperwork. This typically involves signing authority to allow a broker (an intermediary) to trade on your behalf and also some bank account forms and other documentation verifying your identity.

Additionally, you are required to sign some forms to open a share trading account linked to an options trading account. Be sure to use the same brokerage service for your shares and options. This is particularly important with covered calls – the shares you own are used as collateral. If you already have a share account, but you can't tie an options account to it, you will have to set up a new one with a broker who can deal with both options and shares. This means you will have to transfer your shares to them. It doesn't take long – I've helped several people and the paperwork isn't really that daunting. It's worth the effort.

The operations

Selling and buying Put Options

The idea behind this is you (the 'seller') sell put options on shares you would be happy to buy, with the option having a strike price that represents a price you are happy to pay for the stock. If you don't get to buy the stock at a price you're happy with (based on analysis you have undertaken – see below), then you do it again the next month, or move on to another stock if you feel the original one you were looking at is overvalued. Remember, it's not wise to sell puts on a stock that is too far overvalued as they are subject to greater price corrections. Having said that, this can happen even for well-priced stock, but that's not a huge concern because you were happy to buy the stock and you can sell covered calls against it to continue to generate income and reduce the effective cost of purchase. The examples later in this book demonstrate this process in action.

Selling Call Options (Writing covered calls)

As pretty much all investors will be holding stock at some point, this is an important strategy. Most people familiar with options will be aware of covered call writing. This strategy is used on shares you already own and is a low risk, simple and effective strategy that has been used to great effect in the recent market climate. Writing covered calls involved selling call options against your existing shareholdings. You are paid a premium for sclling the call option, which acts as additional income from your shares.

It is important to note that with this strategy, there are certain market conditions in which it can be more or less effective. For instance, the market can either go up, down or sideways. Those are the only ways the market can move. The only real variables are how fast or slow the market moves. Generally, selling covered calls works well in a flat or falling market.

Thanks for choosing this book, if you enjoy it please leave a short review on amazon, I'd really like to know what you think about it

Chapter 2: Trader's Mindset

Trading psychology is the mental state and emotions that determine the success or failure of trading options. It represents the aspect of your behavior that dictates the decisions you make when faced with a trade. Psychology is vital to any business and can do compared to experience, knowledge, and skills in determining your success as a trader.

When you decide to start options trading, you need to grasp the risk-taking concept and discipline that determines the implementation of any trade.

The two most common emotions are greed and fear, while others are regret and hope.

We associate trading psychology to some behaviors and emotions that are often the triggers for catalysts for decisions. The most common feelings that every trader will come across are fear and greed.

Fear

At any given time, fear represents one of the worst kinds of emotions that you can have. Check-in your newspaper one day, and you read about a steep selloff, and the next thing is trying to rack your brain about what to do next, even if it isn't the right action at that time.

Many investors think that they know what will happen in the next few days, which makes them have a lot of confidence in the trade outcome. That leads to investors getting into the trade at a level that is too high or too low, which in turn makes them react emotionally.

As the trader puts a lot of hope on the single trade, the level of fear tends to increase, and hesitation and caution kick in.

Fear is part of every trader, but skilled traders can manage anxiety. There are various types of worries that you will experience, let us look at a few of them:

The Fear to Lose

Have you ever entered a trade, and all you could think about is losing? The fear of losing makes it hard for you to execute the perfect strategy or exit a procedure at the right time.

As a trader, you know that you need to make timely decisions when the strategy signals you to take one. When you be afraid guiding you, the level of confidence drops, and you cannot execute the procedure the right way, at the right time. When a strategy fails, you lose trust in your abilities as well as policy.

When you lose trust in many of the strategies, you end up with analysis paralysis, whereby you cannot pull the trigger on any decision that you make. Making a move becomes a considerable challenge.

When you cannot pull the trigger, you can think about staying away from the pain of losing, while you need to move towards gains.

No trader likes to lose, but it is a fact that even the best traders will make losses occasionally. The key is for them to make more profitable trades that allow them to stay in the game.

When you worry too much, you end up being distracted by your execution process. Instead, you focus on the results.

To reduce the fear of trading, you need to accept losses. The probability of losing or making a profit is 50/50, and you need to take this fact and receive a trade, whether it is a sell or a buy signal.

The Fear of a Positive Trend Going Negative (and Vice Versa)

Many traders choose to go for quick profits and then leave the losses to run down. Many traders want to convince themselves that they have made some money for the day, so they tend to go for a quick profit so that they have the winning feeling.

So, what should you do instead? You need to stick with the trend. When you notice a pattern starts, it is good to stay with the direction until you have a signal that the trend is about to reverse. It is only then that you exit this position.

To understand this concept, you need to consider the history of the market. History is good at pointing out that times change, and trends can go either way. Remember that no one knows the exact time the direction will start or end; all you need to do is waiting upon the signal.

The Fear of Missing Out

For every trade, you have people that doubt the capacity of the business to go through. After you place the market, you will face many skeptics who will challenge the whole procedure and leave you wondering whether to exit the strategy.

This fear is also characterized by greed – because you are not working on the premise of making a successful trade rather the fact that the security is rising without you having a piece of the pie.

This fear usually based on information that there is a trend that you missed that you would have capitalized on.

This fear has a downside – you will forget about any potential risk associated with the trade and instead think that you can make a profit because other people benefited from the action.

Fear of Being Wrong

Many traders put too much emphasis on being right that they forget that this is a business they should run the right way. They also forget that being successful is all about knowing the trend and how it affects their engagement.

When you follow the best timing strategy, you create many positive results over a particular time.

The uncanny desire to focus on always being right instead of focusing on making money is an excellent part of your ego, and to stay on the right path; you need to trade without your ego for once.

If you accommodate a perfectionist mentality when you get into trades, you will be after failure because you will experience a lot of losses. Perfectionists do not take losses the right way, and this translates into fear.

Ways to Overcome Fear in Trading

As you can see, it was evident that fear can lead to losses. So, how can you avoid this fear and become successful?

Learn

You need to find a way to get knowledge so that you have the basis for making decisions. When you know all there is to know about options, you know what to buy and when to sell, and learn which ones to watch. You are then more comfortable making the right decisions.

Envision the bigger picture

You always need to evaluate your choices and see what you have gained or lost to take some steps. Understanding the mistakes, you made guides you to make better decisions in the future.

Start Small

Many traders that subscribe to fear have lost a lot before. They put a lot of funds on the line and ended up losing, which made them fear to place other trades. Begin with small sums so that you do not risk too much to put fear in you. Once you get more confident, you can invest more significant quantities so that you enjoy more profit.

Use the Right Strategy

Having the right trading strategy makes it easy to execute your trades successfully. Make sure you look at various options trading strategies to know which one is ideal for your situation and skills.

Many strategies can help you succeed, but others might leave you confused. If you have a policy that does not give you the returns you desire, adjust it to suit your needs. Refine it till you are comfortable with its performance.

Go Simple

When you have a simple and straightforward strategy, you will be less likely to lose confidence along the way because you know what to expect.

Additionally, the easier the strategy, the faster it will be to spot any issues.

Do Not Hesitate

At times you must jump into the fray even if you are not so comfortable with how it works. Once you begin taking steps, you will learn more about the trade.

However, you always need to be prepared when taking any trade. The more prepared you are, the easier it will be for you to run successful businesses.

Do Not Give Up

Things might not always go as you expect them to do. Remember that mistakes are there to give you lessons that will make you a better trader. When you lose, take time to identify the error you made, correct it, and then try again.

Greed

That refers to a selfish desire to get more money than you need from a trade. When the desire to get more than you can usually make takes over your decision-making process, you are looking at failure.

Greed does seem to be more detrimental than fear. Fear can make you lose trades, but the good thing is that you get to preserve your capital. On the other hand, greed places you in a situation where you spend your wealth faster than you return. It pushes you to act when you should not be acting at all.

The Danger of Being Greedy

When you are greedy, you end up acting irrationally. Irrational trading behavior can be overtrading, overleveraging, holding onto trades for too long, or chasing different markets.

The more greed you have, the more foolish you act. If you reach a point at which desire takes over from common sense, you are overdoing it.

When you are greedy, you also end up risking much more than

you can handle, and you end up with a loss. You also have unrealistic expectations from the market, which makes it seem like you are after just money and nothing else.

When you are greedy, you also start trading prematurely without any knowledge of the options trading market.

When you are too greedy, your judgment is clouded. You will not think about any harmful consequences that might result when you make confident decisions.

Many traders that were too greedy ended up giving up after making this mistake in the initial trading phase.

How to Overcome Greed

Like any other endeavor in trading, you need a lot of effort to overcome greed. It might not be easy because we are talking about human emotions here, but it is possible.

First, you must know that every call you make will always not be the right one. There are times when you will not make the right move, and you will end up losing money. At times you will miss the perfect strategy altogether, and you will not move a step ahead.

Secondly, you must agree that the market is way bigger than you. When you do this, you will accept and make mistakes in the process.

Hope

Hope is what keeps a trading expectation alive when it has reached reversal. Hope usually factored in the mind of a trader that has placed a considerable amount on a trade. Many traders also go for hope when they wish to recoup past losses. These traders are always hopeful that the next business will be the best, and they end up placing more than they should on the business.

This type of emotion is dangerous because it does not care at all about your hopes and will take your money.

Chapter 3: Long Call Strategy

If you were first to open your contract by selling, we say that you are "short." If you buy to open a position, we assume that you are "long." The simplest way to trade options is to take a faraway place on a call or a put. Although when buying and selling stocks, we say that someone "shorts" the capital when they are hoping to profit off a decline in share price, you can be expecting to profit from a reduction in share price, you are "long" concerning the put option.

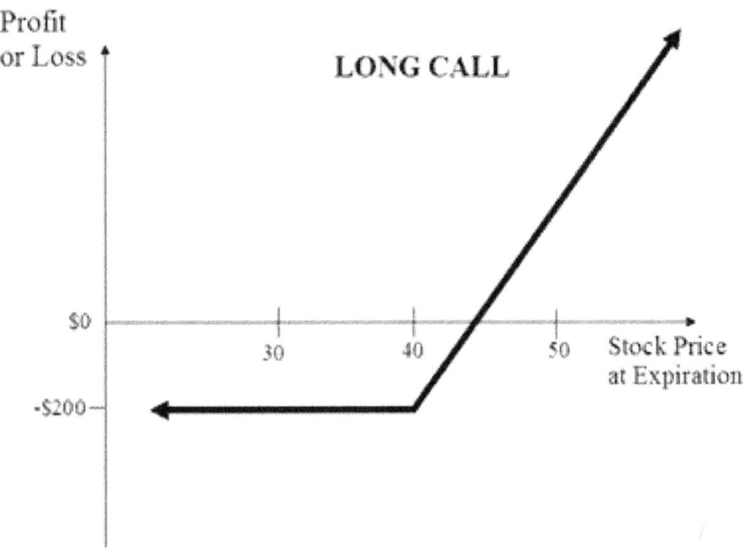

The strategy for profiting from going long on a call or put option is simple. You are hoping the stock price would move in your favor so that you will earn a profit. The industry is full of naysayers that downplay this basic strategy. However, the reality is you can make profits in this way. That is buying or selling individual options, be they the call or put variety. When doing this type of trading, the key to success is to stay on top of it and don't buy options on a whim. You need a good reason to buy a call or a put option by itself. That means paying attention to the financial news surrounding the company, earnings reports, and looking at simple market trends to determine when you have a reasonable probability of earning a profit.

Day Trading and Options

This is just an aside, but watching the movement of a stock price over a single day can provide opportunities to ride a short-term trend in cost and profit handsomely. Rising and falling share prices are magnified in the amount of the option, so when the share price goes up a few tens of cents, you might profit by $65 or $75 in a single day.

But be aware that the rules for day trading apply to options as well. To be a day trader approved by your broker in the United States, you need to have a margin account. It needs to have $25,000 deposited in the statement. Since options trading often takes place on the level of tens or hundreds of dollars, the vast majority of beginning options traders are not going to be looking to be a day trader. But you are going to be tempted to get out of some trades on the same day that you enter the profession because you might have ridden a trend in one direction or the other to significant profits. The trend might not continue the following day, and you don't want to eat some of your earnings from the theta or time decay.

The rule you need to be aware of is that if you make four-day trades over five days, you will be labeled a pattern day trader. To keep your account open, you'd have to fund it with $25,000. So, this is a situation that you are probably going to want to avoid. To avoid being pulled under by this, simply limit the number of day trades to 3 per week.

Remember that the five-day rule means five consecutive trading days, so weekends don't count. If you made a day trade on Friday, the following Monday, that day, business still counts against you.

Call Options Basic Strategy

The basic strategy behind making profits with call options is to buy low and sell high. You can profit from this strategy by riding a single day's price movements or "swing trading" the opportunity over one or more days, meaning that you will hold the option overnight. You are not going to keep the option until expiration unless you intend to buy the stock.

The time to sell the option is when you have made an acceptable level of profits. You should set this level beforehand so that you do not let the emotions of the moment rule your decisions. It's not uncommon to make $50 or $100 profits in a few days or a single day off one option contract. Still, many traders get dollar signs in their eyes – they get overcome with greed – and as a result, they hold their positions too long. That can mean lost profits, defeat by time decay, or even seeing the option wiped out.

One lesson that you are going to learn is that options prices can fluctuate dramatically. This is because the underlying stock is 100 shares. So, a small change in the stock price is magnified by 100 for your investment in the option. Using a one-to-one pricing relationship for simplicity, if the cost of the stock moves up by a mere 45 cents, the price of the option will go up by $45. On the other hand, if it drops by 30 cents, the amount of choice would lose $30.

Although the situation of using one-to-one pricing is not realistic, it's pretty clear that small price changes in stock mean significant price changes in your investment.

The key to success with trading options is to have a trading plan that you follow, and which has specific rules. We will cover that at the end of the chapter.

One skill you are going to need to develop when it comes to calling options is reading stock charts. The details of this are beyond the scope of this book, and you can learn about it online or purchase a book on day trading. There are three necessary skills that I recommend you have:

- Learn how to read and interpret candlestick charts.

- Learn how to use moving averages.

- Learn how to use and interpret Bollinger bands.

Let's briefly discuss each of these in turn. A candlestick chart divides a stock chart into time intervals that you specify. The time interval you are going to use will depend on the time frame over which you are hoping to trade. I have had some success trading call options using a buy to open strategy. I can't say what the situation is in all cases, but I will tell you that I don't stay in these trades very long. What I do is I check the early morning financial news for any surprises. Then when the market opens, I look for early indicators of how it's going to move.

If the other aspects of the stock look good – that is, I can buy options with a high level of open interest – then I will enter a position if it seems like there is going to be a strong move over the day or the next few days.

Let's give a few specific examples so that you will have some practical advice for the situation. You can trade index funds like the Dow Jones Industrial Average (trade options on DIA), the S & P 500 (trade options on SPY), or the NASDAQ (trade options on QQQ). These index funds are susceptible to general economic and political news. If you see that a good jobs report has come out, that is a good signal to get in on one or more of these funds. It's often worth the risk to get in on options for these index funds the day before. Then you can wake up and see the results. It's going to be possible to double an investment overnight. Since you are not day trading, in that case, it's a simple matter to exit your positions for a profit. But keep in mind, there is a risk as well if it works against you (we will discuss strategies to use to cover both movements). If you buy a call, but the early indication is a market sell-off, then get rid of the put first thing when the market opens.

This is an excellent example of why open interest is essential to look at. If you were to buy an option on something with a small level of public interest, you might not be able to get rid of your options before the put lost a lot of money. With something that is very heavily traded like SPY, however, it's a sure bet that you can unload the put quickly.

You also want to pay attention to news about specific companies. For example, if there is news coming out in the early morning hours that the government is going to investigate the social media companies, that is a good indication that going long on a put option would be a reasonable strategy. Conversely, recently, the FTC announced a settlement with Facebook, and this sent the stock soaring.

You are not going to be getting the news "first" as an individual retail investor. Still, the good news is that with options trading, if you are staying on top of things, you will be able to get in and out of your trades and take profits if you are careful about it.

Reading the Charts

As an options trader, you are going to have to learn how to read charts. The first thing to do is look up candlestick patterns to recognize when a trend reversal might become. Candlestick patterns are not absolute rules or truth-tellers; they are an indicator. You consider the candlestick charts and use the entirety of the information you have available to make your decisions.

As we said earlier, a candlestick can be divided into different timeframes. If you are looking to ride a trend over a single day, a five-minute timeline is reasonable to use. In this case, each candlestick will tell you what the price action was over five minutes.

The candlesticks are going to be colored green or red. If a candlestick is green, it's a "bullish" candlestick. That means that the closing price had risen to a more considerable higher than the opening price throughout the interest. By itself, it does not tell you where the price is headed. For a bullish candlestick, the top of the candle is the price at the end of the trading session, and the bottom of the body is the price at the start.

Each candlestick has "wicks" that come out of the top and bottom of the menorah. The top wick gives you a high price for the time interval. The bottom candlestick gives you a low estimate of the time interval.

If a candlestick is red, that is a "bearish" candlestick. In that case, this means that the closing price was lower than the opening price. So, the top of the body is the opening price in this case, and the bottom of the body is the closing price (the price closed lower than it opened at). The meaning of wicks is the same.

A complete investigation of candlesticks is beyond this book's scope, so please see online resources or books specifically addressing the topic, or day trading, to learn the patterns that you need to be looking for. That said, here are the general rules for entering and exiting trades. In the event of big news that you know will cause a massive move in the share price, you want to get in early in the trading day.

Options Trading Graph:

Chapter 4: Covered Call Strategy

In this chapter, we'll investigate a trading strategy that is an excellent way to get started selling options for beginners. This strategy called covered calls. By covered, we mean that you've got an asset that includes the potential sale of the underlying stocks. In other words, you already own the shares of stocks. Now, why would you want to write a call option on stocks you already own? The basis of this strategy is that you don't expect the stock price to move very much during the lifetime of the options contract, but you want to generate money over the short term in the form of premiums that you can collect. That can help you create a short-term income stream; you must structure your calls carefully.

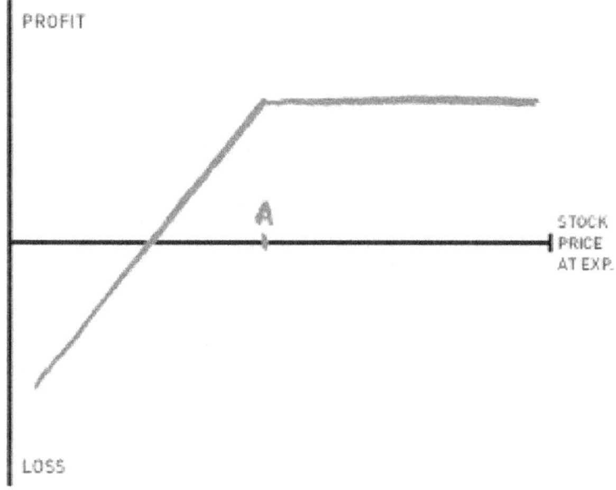

Setting up covered calls is relatively low risk and will help you get familiar with many of the aspects of options trading. While it's probably not going to make you productive overnight, it's an excellent way to learn the trade tools.

Covered Calls involve an extended position.

To create a covered call, you need to own at least 100 shares of stock in one underlying equity. When you create a request, you're going to be offering potential buyers a chance to buy these shares from you. Of course, the strategy is that you're only going to sell high, but your real goal is to get the income stream from the premium.

The premium is a one-time non-refundable fee. If a buyer purchases your call option and pays you the premium, that money is yours. No matter what happens after that, you've got that cash to keep. If the stock doesn't reach the strike price, the contract will expire, and you can create a new call option on the same underlying shares. Of course, if the stock price does pass the strike price, the buyer of the contract will probably exercise their right to buy the shares. You will still earn money on the trade, but the risk is you're giving up the potential to make as much money that could have collected on the business.

You write a covered call option that has a strike price of $67. Suppose that for some unforeseen reason, the shares skyrocket to $90 a share. The buyer of your call option will be able to purchase the shares from you at $67. So, you've gained $2 a share. However, you've missed out on selling the shares at a profit of $35 a share. Instead, the investor who purchased the call option from you will turn around and sell the shares on the markets for the actual spot price, and they will reap the benefits.

However, you haven't lost anything. You have earned the premium plus sold your shares of stock for a modest profit.

That risk – that the stocks will rise to a much higher price than the strike price - always exists, but if you do your homework, you're going to be offering shares that you don't expect to change much in price over the lifetime of your call. So, suppose instead that the price only rose to $68. The amount exceeded the strike price so the buyer may exercise their option. In that case, you are still missing out on some profit that you could have had otherwise, but it's a small amount, and we're not taking into account the premium.

If the stock price doesn't exceed the strike price over the contract's length, you get to keep the premium and get to keep the shares. The dividend is yours to keep no matter what.

In reality, in most situations, a covered call is going to be a win-win situation for you.

Covered Calls are a Neutral Strategy
A covered call is known as a "neutral" strategy. Investors create covered calls for stocks in their portfolio, where they only expect small moves over the lifetime of the contract. Moreover, investors will use covered calls on stocks that they plan to hold for the long term. It's a way to earn money on the shares during a period in which the investor expects that the stock won't move much at a price and have no earning potential from selling.

An Example of a Covered Call

Let's say that you own 100 shares of Acme Communications. It's currently trading at $40 a share. Over the next several months, nobody expects the stock to move very much, but as an investor, you feel Acme Communications has substantial long-term growth potential. To make a little bit of money, you sell a call option on Acme Communications with a strike price of $43. Suppose that the premium is $0.78 and that the call option lasts three months.

For 100 shares, you'll earn a total premium payment of $0.78 x 100 = $78. No matter what happens, you pocket the $78.

Now let's say that over the next three months, the stock drops a bit in price so that it never comes close to the strike price, and at the end of the three months, it's trading at $39 a share.

The options contract will expire, and it's worthless. The buyer of the options contract ends up empty-handed. You have a win-win situation. You've earned the extra $78 per 100 shares, and you still own your shares at the end of the contract.

Now let's say that the stock does increase a bit in value. Over time, it jumps up to $42, and then to $42.75, but then drops down to $41.80 by the time the options contract expires. In this scenario, you're finding yourself in a much better position. In this case, the strike price of $43 never reached, so the buyer of the call option again left out. On the other hand, you keep the premium of $78, and you still get to keep the shares of stock. This time since the shares have increased in value, you're a lot better off than you were before, so it's a win-win situation for YOU, even though it's a sad situation for the poor soul who purchased your call.

Sadly, there is another possibility that the stock price exceeds the strike price before the contract expires. In that case, we required to sell the stock. You still end up in a position that isn't all that bad, however. You didn't lose any actual money, but you lost a potential profit. You still get the premium of $78, plus the earnings from the sale of the 100 shares at the strike price of $43.

A covered call is almost a zero-risk situation because you never actually lose money even though if the stock price soars, you missed out on an opportunity. You can minimize that risk by choosing stocks you use for a covered call option carefully. For example, if you hold shares in a pharmaceutical company that rumored to be announcing a cure for cancer in two months, you probably don't want to use those shares for a covered call. A company with more long-term prospects but probably isn't going anywhere in the next few months is a better bet.

How to go about creating a covered call

To create a covered call, you'll need to own 100 shares of stock. While you don't want to risk a capital that is likely to take off shortly, you don't want to pick a total dud. There is always someone willing to buy something – at the right price. But you want to go with a decent stock so that you can earn a modest premium.

You start by getting online at your brokerage and looking up the stock online. When you look up stocks online, you'll be able to look at their "option chain," which will give you information from a table on premiums available for calls on this stock. You can see these listed under bid price. The bid price presented on a per-share basis, but a call contract has 100 shares. If your bid price is $1.75, then the actual premium you're going to get is $1.75 x 100 = $175.

An important note is that the further out the expiration date, the higher the premium. A good rule of thumb is to pick an expiry between two and three months from the present time. Remember that the longer you go, the higher the risk because that increases the odds that the stock price will exceed the strike price, and you'll end up having to sell the shares.

You have an option (no pun intended) with the premium you want to charge. Theoretically, you can set any price you want. Of course, that requires a buyer willing to pay that price for you to make money. A more reasonable strategy is to look at prices people are currently requesting for call options on this stock. You can do this by checking the asking price for the call options on the stock. You can also see prices that buyers are currently offering by looking at the bid prices. For an immediate sale, you can simply set your price to a bid price already out there. If you want to go a little bit higher, you can submit the order and then wait until someone comes along to buy your call option at the bid price.

To sell a covered call, you select "sell to open."

Benefits of Covered Calls

A covered call is a relatively low-risk option. The worst-case scenario is that you'll be out of your shares but earn a small profit, a more modest profit than you could have made if you had not created the call contract and simply sold your shares. However, you also get the premium.

A covered call allows you to generate income from your portfolio in the form of premiums.

If you don't expect any price moves on the stock in the near term and plan on holding it a long time, it's a reasonable strategy to generate income without taking much risk.

Risks of Covered Calls

Covered calls can be a risk if you're bullish on the stock, and your expectations realized, and there is a price spike. In that case, you've traded the small amount of income of the premium with a voluntary cap of the strike price for the potential upside you could have had if you had simply held the stock and sold it at a high cost.

If the stock price plummets, while you still get the premium, the stocks will be worthless unless they rebound over the long term. You shouldn't use a call option on stocks that you expect to be on the path to a significant drop in the coming months. In that case, rather than writing a covered call, you should simply sell the stocks and take your losses. Alternatively, you can continue holding the shares to see if they rebound over the long term.

Chapter 5: Protective Put Strategy

This is a bit different, so let's consider how a placed option works. In the case of a put option, we are looking for a proportion charge to drop. Of direction, the person promoting a positioned alternative is hoping that the percentage rate isn't going to shoot low sufficient to be relevant to their replacement. But if it does drop that a lot, the customer of the option has the proper to sell stocks at the strike charge. So, let's say that this share price drops from $90 a percentage to $50 a share, and the strike price is $80. So, the proprietor of the placed option should purchase one hundred shares at $50 a proportion. Then they can work out the option and sell the stocks on the strike price of $80. That would provide them an income of $30 consistent with percentage.

So that's an overview of what a placed option is if you weren't specified. So, let's talk approximately promoting an included put. When you encourage a positioned option, you are banking on the proportion price staying high. Thus, developing a put option is a bullish move. Buying a put alternative is a bearish move.

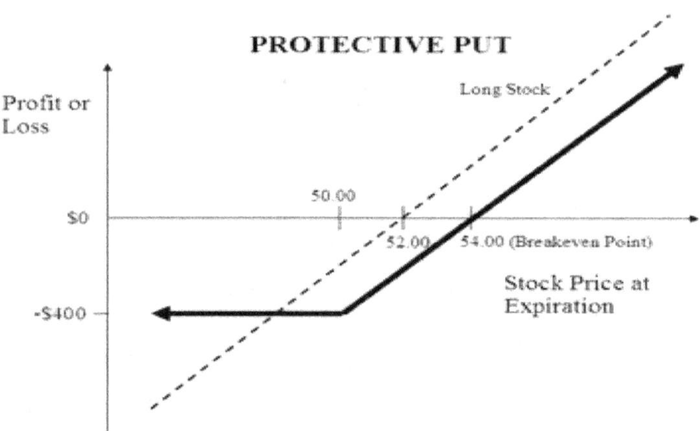

Selling a positioned option is pretty a hazard if it ends up getting exercised. So, you have to be able to shop for the shares if they are "placed" to you. That can amount to a large amount of money. For this purpose, brokerages aren't all that demanding to let humans sell positioned options.

To sell a covered place, you have to put the cash that could be required inside the occasion the option was exercised to buy the stocks. So, if the strike charge is $50, you need to have 100 x $50 = $5000 for your account to cover the positioned alternative. That way, if it's exercised, you'll be able to do it and no longer get the broking in trouble. In exchange for this, you might make $ 100 selling the position.

But there are lots you may do with $5000, so I am now not positive why every person might trouble to tie up all their capital to make this sort of small quantity of earnings. You may additionally as properly have placed it inside the financial institution for that short amount of money. As a minimum, you won't be at risk of buying a hundred shares of stock.

Put Options as Insurance

Some readers can be questioning why you have got placed alternatives apart from gambling. The actual cause that set options to existing is to provide insurance. That is, the vendor of a placed choice is assuming the risk with a stock. Many big players buy placed options to insure their stock against catastrophic losses. So, if you purchase a put option with a strike charge of $50, that limits any possible chance you have in keeping the stock so that you don't end up losing that extra $50 a share if the stock went to zero. The vendor of the positioned alternative agrees to buy the stocks at $50. If the stock charge virtually did drop to $0, then the vendor of the placed options has taken at the chance and absorbed the loss for the other party. That is why while you sell put alternatives, and people say which you are selling "top class." This is insurance premiums.

Selling covered positioned options is a waste of your cash. If you had the considerable quantity of capital required to sell a protected placed alternative, you'd be tying uploads of money so one can make a couple of hundred bucks.

Selling Naked Puts

Selling naked put options is one of the most famous methods to earn a profit from alternatives. In this method, you don't have to keep all of the money required to cover the sale of stock at the strike fee in your account. Instead, the first thing you do is open a margin account.

Remember, a margin account is an account that can be used to borrow money from a dealer. In this example, brokerages can have components that they use to decide the amount of money that you want to have to your account. It's going to depend upon the option's strike price, the present-day share rate, and some different factors. Each brokerage may additionally do it a touch bit differently. So, you should test along with your brokerage to see what the particular rule is.

The amount of cash required will be tons smaller than what might be needed for a covered place. However, you are still going to have many thousand bucks as much as maybe $10,000 on the way to make a living doing this.

So, the first part of the strategy that many human beings make is that you are going to sell placed options far out of the cash. You need to decrease the possibility that they are going to be exercised. So, for example, in case you sell a put agreement with a delta of 0.22, there may be only a 22% threat of the options going in the cash by way of expiration. So, disturbing approximately assignment is moot.

In each man or woman case, you'll have to check the volume and open hobby to decide whether or no longer it's worth selling a particular alternative. But in this approach, there is no shopping for on your component going on. If you observe the method, all you have been doing is selling options premium. This is crucial to emphasize that for beginners, the concept of being worried inside the stock marketplace without shopping for something is a new way to consider things.

Many massive hit investors do nothing but promote placed alternatives. You can, without difficulty, make $1 million 12 months doing it. Some of the recommendation used in the different sections applies here as nicely. So, you don't need to be targeting too many groups because you want to be correctly informed approximately what's going on. Among different matters, every week, you want to evaluate your danger of being assigned. That means cautiously tracking the percentage rate of every stock. As we counseled earlier, you don't need your attention to spread too thin.

We also need to keep in mind the expiration dates of the alternatives that we promote. If we go out 30 to forty-five days, in preference to selling options that are going to expire quickly, we will earn plenty more super-premium from the sale. Of route, this is assuming that the possibilities are going to run out of the cash. But if the whole thing is chosen cautiously, there is a good chance that matters are going to paintings in your favor. You can assume that to take place around 70% of the time.

Some investors do matters differently, however. This is honestly going to sound acquainted due to the fact we discussed a similar problem. So, in this situation, what you could do is you can sell options that expire within a week or much less. The change-off with this method is that you're going to get paid a lower top rate. But if the options are out of the money, over per week, it doesn't have very long left to live. What meaning is there's going to be considerable time decay, and that brings us to the possibility of the options expiring worthless. Or you can buy it lower back the day earlier than expiration for pennies at the dollar. And this happens truly rapidly over the direction of 1 week. Every week, you will set up sufficient options to make whatever profits you had in mind and promote them off. Hopefully, they might sell quickly because, with the week, you don't have tons' time to clutter around.

From here, it's a rely upon merely looking at the options to make sure there isn't any chance that they turn out to be inside the money.

Selling bare positioned alternatives is one in every of the most popular techniques utilized by experienced alternatives traders. It's pretty low danger, and it brings a regular profit. You can effortlessly make 1,000,000 bucks a yr. from it in case you build up over time. The most effective requirement is you are going to need to set up a margin account because of this depositing $2,000 at least. To get an idea of what is required to make $2,000 a week using tasty works promoting positive positioned alternatives, I'd need to deposit $11,000. That might be an entirely fundamental tradeoff, you're just preserving the $11,000 in the account, and every week, you sell $2,000 worth of options, and now you've got annual earnings of around $104,000.

Selling Naked Call Options

Since we've been talking about approximately selling put options, it's not going to be a wonder that the next strategy is to promote bare name alternatives. But this exposes the beauty of other options once again. While each person else is panicking to determine whether the stock market goes up or down, as an alternatives dealer, it doesn't be counted. To clarify this, I will let you know that promoting naked positioned options is a strategy used in a bull market. Since stock expenses are rising, it makes me feel about selling opportunities, which are unlikely to be exercised. The stock price is in no way going to drop down that far.

Conversely, assume the market is in a downturn. That might make selling placed options less attractive and probably enhance the threat of doing so. This is in which call options come to our rescue. If it was 2008 and the stock market became tanking, in place of being a part of the frenzied promote-off, you could be promoting name options.

And there's absolutely no worry, after all, study all the individuals who are shopping for put alternatives now that are far out of the cash, even though the stock market is on a rising route that never seems to end. So, if the market becomes going the other course, you will find human beings, who, for whatever motive that simplest they realize, would be willing to buy call alternatives underneath one's circumstances.

So as an alternatives dealer, you have to be flexible. And which means being prepared to move in among selling name alternatives and put alternatives as the situation demands. Of path, you could apply the different techniques that we discussed earlier, so, for example, you may sell name credit score spreads while the marketplace is in a downturn.

Selling a naked call is identical to promoting an open position as a way of the basic ideas. But in this example, we are hoping that the proportion charge doesn't upward thrust above our strike price. You'll also need to have a few collateral stages on your account, similar to the case with the naked positioned options. The standards other than that might be the same. So, if you're in an undergo market, you will be selling out of the cash call options and pocketing the income each week. While the market hit backside and started out reversing ending the recession, then you definitely could alternate your technique and go back to promoting naked positioned alternatives.

Chapter 6: Iron, Short Condor and Calendar Spread

Iron Condor

An even more fascinating strategy will be the iron condor. The names of some option strategies can be very visceral: strips, spreads, splits, strangles, straddles, puts, and calls. If there was ever a strategy named out of sci-fantasy, it is the IRON CONDOR. In most option books, the iron condor is tucked away in a final chapter written for veteran, seasoned, experienced, battle-tested option traders. Before computers, online trading, and highly sophisticated trading platforms became common, I might have agreed to hide this strategy on a back page, but not anymore.

If you trade a Put spread and Call spread at the same time, we call it an IRON CONDOR. The iron condor is built by offering one out-of-the-money put and purchasing one out-of-the-money put associated with a reduced hit (bull put spread), plus promoting one out-of-the-money call and purchasing one out-of-the-money call of a more significant hit (bear call spread). All choices have precisely the same expiration date and are on a similar underlying asset. Generally, the put, as well as call sides, have precisely the same spread width. This particular trading tactic earns a total premium on the structure, and it is created to make use of a stock experiencing very low volatility. Many traders this way trade because of its perceived high probability of making a tiny amount of premium.

In the P& L graph, notice how the optimum gain is created once the stock stays in a somewhat vast trading range, which could lead to the investor making the entire net credit received when producing the trade. The further the inventory moves from the short strikes (lower for the put, more significant for the call), the higher the damage up with the optimum loss. Optimum damage usually is considerably more considerable compared to the maximum gain, which intuitively makes good sense, given that there's a higher likelihood of the framework finishing with a little gain.

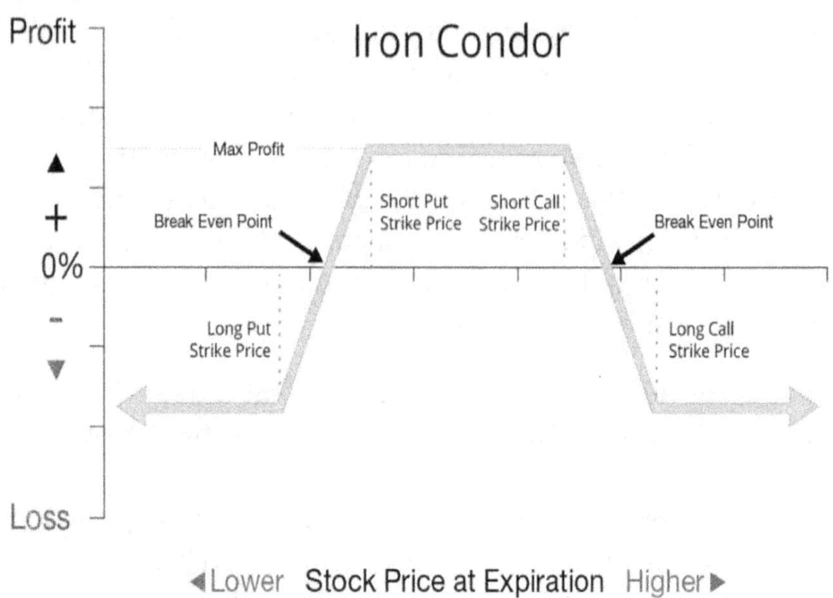

The Condor Spread

The Condor Spread Strategy is a more complex, yet highly effective trading strategy, especially for those traders whose primary focus is in generating income.

The Condor spread is a limited risk, non-directional trading strategy that is designed to earn a profit when the underlying security is more stagnant or range bound in its behavior.

Using call options with the same expiration month, a trader can structure a long condor spread by buying (long) a lower in-the-money call, writing a higher strike at-the-money call, writing another even higher at-the-money call, and buying an even higher out-of-the-money call. A total of four legs are involved in the condor options strategy and a net debit is required to establish the position.

The maximum profit for the long condor strategy is realized when the stock closes between the two middle strikes at expiration. The maximum risk for the long condor strategy is simply the debit paid to enter the trade. Because of the four leg position there are actually two different break-even price points that can be determined.

One of the most powerful reasons the Condor Spread is utilized is the ability to profit from a non-directional move in the underlying stock.

The Condor Spread Explained

The Condor spread is a way to profit from a non-directional move in an underlying security while reducing the risk and cost of time and volatility.

Suppose XYZ stock is trading at $30. An options trader enters a call condor trade by buying (long) a front month 20 call for $10.25, writing (short) a front month 25 call for $5.50, writing (short) another front month 35 call for $1.00, and buying (long) another front month 40 call for $0.25.

Max Profit

The condor spread has a max profit potential just like the four vertical spreads (bull call, bull put, bear, call bear put). In the above example the most you can possibly make is $1.00 per share from the trade as long as XYZ closes above $24 and below $36 on expiration.

Max Loss

The condor spread has a max loss potential as well. If the stock closes above $36 or below $24 on expiration the net debit spent would be lost.

What could happen?

Just like every other strategy we have and will discuss there are three potential outcomes for this trade. The underlying stock could move up in price, down in price or stay the same.

Let's evaluate the results across all three scenarios. Suppose you buy (long) a front month $20 call for $10.25, write (short) a front month $25 call for $5.50, write (short) another front month $35 call for $1.00, and buy (long) another front month $40 call for $0.25.

Remember our stock price was $30.00. The debit spent in the condor will be $4.00 because you paid $10.25 for the $20 call, $0.25 for the $40 call, and you collected $5.50 from the sale of the $25 call and $1.00 from the $35 call ($10.25 − $5.50 − $1.00 + $0.25 = $4.00).

How does the condor perform in our usual three scenarios: the "up" scenario, the "down" scenario and the "stagnant" scenario?

Due to the inherent structure of this trade we are actually giving the stock room to move around. This allows us to take advantage of a stocks natural support and resistance as well as its pre-determined trading range. Ideally we would prefer the stock not move much in either direction, however, this trade gives us room to breathe.

With the stock currently trading at $30, this trade allows for a trading range between $24 and $36. In truth as long as the stock closes above $24 and below $36 on expiration, this trade will produce a profit.

The simplest way for one to understand the risks and rewards of this strategy is to **break it down to its core components: An In-the-money Bull Call Spread and an Out-of-the-money Bear Call spread.**

Basically what we have is a long $20 strike call and a short $25 Strike call (Bull Call Spread) with a **net debit of $4.75.**

We also have a long $40 strike call and a short $35 strike call (Bear Call Spread) for a **net credit of $0.75**

The combined position gives us a Condor Spread with a net debit of $4.00 ($4.75 - $0.75)

Now that we are clear on what we have let's discuss what can happen in each of the three directional scenarios.

If the stock moves down from $30:

If our stock begins to move down in price from $30 our primary focus will be on the bull call spread (L20C, S25C). The reason we would not be concerned with the bear call spread (L40C, S35C) is because the stock is already below our short $35 call strike. Since it is below the $35 call strike both the $35 and $40 calls will expire worthless and we will get to keep the entire $0.75 credit we received upon entry.

Our risk comes into play from the bull call spread which was a net debit trade to enter. So for teaching purposes let's suppose the bottom falls out of our stock and it declines from $30 down to $20. If the stock drops to $20 on expiration day what happens to the Bear Call spread? Remember, the $40 strike call and the $35 strike call will expire worthless and we will keep our $0.75 credit.

However, what happens to our Bull Call spread when the stock is at $20? Well the short $25 strike call will expire worthless (no one wants to purchase the stock from us at $25 when it is currently trading at $20) and our $20 strike call expires worthless. Since both options expire worthless we will lose the $4.75 we spent to enter the trade, bringing our net loss to $4.00 ($4.75 - $0.75).

What if the stock closes at $15? We would still experience the net $4.00 loss because all the options would expire worthless and we would keep the $0.75 credit from our Bear Call spread and lose the $4.75 from our Bull Call spread giving us a net $4.00 loss.

Let's suppose XYZ closes at $30 on expiration. If that is the case what happens to our Bull Call Spread? What happens to our Bear Call Spread? What happens to our overall Condor position?

Let's examine the Bull Call first. If XYZ closes at $30 our $20/$25 Bull Call Spread options will close in-the-money. Our long $20 strike call will have $10.00 of intrinsic value and our short $25 call will have $5.00 of intrinsic value. Therefore if we are long $10 of value and short $5 of value our net position is $5.00 and if we originally spent $4.75 to enter the position our net gain is $0.25 (higher strike call – lower strike call – net debit = profit).

If XYZ closes at $30 our $40/$35 Bear Call Spread options will close out-of-the-money and expire worthless. Since both the long and short options expire worthless we get to keep our original net credit from entry or $0.75.

Therefore if we profit $0.25 from the Bull Call side and $0.75 from the Bear Call side our net gain (if XYZ closes at $30) is $1.00.

In truth, as long as XYZ remains above $25 and Below $35 on

expiration we will profit the $1.00 ($0.25 from the Bull Call side and $0.75 from the Bear Call side).

Using the same prices as the previous example we will now take a look at the "up" scenario. Let's set the stock price at $40.00 on expiration.

At this price both the Bull Call Spread side and the Bear Call Spread side are in the money.

If the Bull Call side is in the money what happens? The long $20 strike call will have $20 of intrinsic value and the short $25 call will have $15 of intrinsic value. If we have $20 of long intrinsic value and $15 of short intrinsic value our net is $5 of intrinsic value minus the $4.75 debit we spent to enter the trade our profit is $0.25.

If the Bear Call spread is in the money what happens? The Long $40 strike call is at-the-money and worthless (on expiration) and the short $35 call is In-the-money and has $5.00 of intrinsic value. Since we are short $5.00 of intrinsic value we will experience a loss. Our loss however is limited to the net debit spent.

How?

We will gain $0.25 from the Bull Call side and we will gain $0.75 from the original credit received on the Bear Call side, however, we are short $5.00 of intrinsic value from the short $35 strike call. Therefore the net maximum loss is $5.00 (intrinsic value) - $0.25 (from the bull call side) - $0.75 (credit from the bear call side) = $4.00 net loss.

Short Condor Spread
You are free to adjust the strike prices of the options you execute for optimizing your preferences of profitability along

with the breakeven ranges. Only use this strategy after you gained some experience as an options trader. There are four transactions you required to execute in a short condor spread. You can use either calls or spreads, but in this example, we'll talk about using calls. Once again, the principle of execution stays the same regardless of it being a call or a put option. The first transaction you are required to execute is right deep in the money calls, and the second transaction is to purchase in the money calls at a higher strike price than the previous calls. The third transaction is to write far out of the money calls and then purchase out of the money calls at a lower strike price than the previous one. The number of options in each set of sale and purchase must be the same along with the expiration date. The only decision you required to make is related to the strike price you use. The potential of your profitability depends on the strike price you use. The more significant is the difference between the strikes and the current price; the higher is your potential to earn a profit. If this range of difference is high, then the strategy is known as a short albatross spread.

Time/Calendar Spread

The last two strategies involved options with the same expiration date, but here it is going to be different. In this strategy, an option with a specified expiration date is purchased, and then it is sold at another expiration date. What remains the same in both these cases is the strike price. The core idea of this strategy is to take full advantage of the factor of time decay.

CALENDAR CALL SPREAD

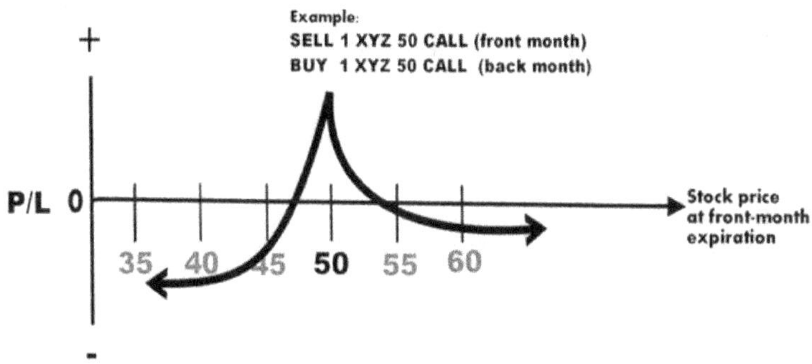

Description: Sell a CALL in front month with about 30 days until expiration, and buy a CALL at the same strike in the next month out. (SAME strike calendar spreads are called horizontal, using a higher strike would make this a diagonal spread). Notice the chart shows P/L at the expiration of the front month option.

The outlook at placing this trade is a steady to slightly bearish move in the underlying. At the expiration of the front month, the trader can liquidate the back month CALL, or some traders look at this trade as a way to purchase the back month CALL at a reduced price; the latter is more often the objective. If this strategy works, the underlying is at or below the front strike and this front month option expires worthless, and the trader might keep the back month option to hold for gains as the underlying rises.

Increasing volatility (IV%) would have the back month increasing faster than the front month (all else being equal). Time-decay works in favor of this trade as the front month has a short time until expiration.

This CALENDAR CALL SPREAD is among the simplest

configurations of CALENDAR SPREADS. Since various strikes can be used and they can be many short and long combinations for both horizontal and diagonal spreads – there are many combinations possible. Quick advice to beginners is do NOT use CALENDAR SPREADS; the nuance of various types of calendar spreads can be complex. For these reasons, this is the only calendar spread illustration in this book.

Chapter 7: Straddles and Strangles

Doing this requires some attention on your part. You are going to have to think ahead to implement this strategy and profit from it. Remember that you can use a straddle or strangle any time that you consider the stock is going to make a significant shift one way or the other. An example of a non-earning season situation, where this could be a useful strategy, would be a new product announcement. Think Apple. If Apple is having one of their big presentations, if the new phone that comes out disappoints analysts, share prices will probably drop by a significant amount. On the other hand, if it ends up surprising viewers with many new features that make it the must-have phone again, this will send Apple stock soaring.

The problem here is you don't know which way it's going to go. There will be leaks and rumors, but basing your trading decisions on that is probably not the right approach; often, the suggestions are wrong. A strangle or straddle you to avoid that kind of situation and make money either way.

Other situations that could make this useful include changes in management or any political interaction. We mentioned the government recently made a privacy settlement with Facebook. If you knew when the arrangement was going to occur but wasn't sure what it was going to be, using a strangle or straddle might be an excellent way to earn money from the significant price moves that were sure to follow.

The same events that might warrant buying a long call, such as a GDP number or jobs report, for options on index funds, are also appropriate for strangles and straddles.

Implied Volatility Strategy

Implied volatility is significant when a big event like an

earnings report is coming. That gives you a way to make profits. We are going to call this the implied volatility strategy.

Let's review how this would work. Remember, implied volatility is a projection of the stock's volatility is going to be short. When there is an earnings call, the volatility will be extreme on the day after the call. Therefore, you are going to see the implied volatility growing as earnings day approaches.

At the time I am writing this, it is 24 hours before Facebook's earnings call. The implied volatility is 74%, which is very high. In contrast, for Apple, which is more than a week away from its next earnings call, the implied volatility is 34%. That is for a $207.50 strike put, with a share price of $207.9.

The strategy is to profit from the implied volatility. You want to enter your position one to two weeks before the earnings call or big announcement. As implied volatility increases, this will swamp out time decay and cause a significant rise in the option price.

Using that Apple put option if we assumed that there were only four days to expiration. Still, the implied volatility had risen to about where Facebook is. There were no other changes (so we will leave the share price where it was), the amount of the put option would increase by about $330.

So, if nothing else, you could profit from the change of implied volatility. It will probably go highest the day before the earnings call.

That is going to continue magnified if you trade a strangle or straddle. Before the earnings call, both the put and the call option are going to increase a great deal in value because of implied volatility. So, you could sell the strangle the day before the earnings call and book some profits then. Since a strangle or straddle can earn big profits if there is a significant move in the share price, you won't find any problems locating a buyer.

Estimating Price from Implied Volatility

If you know the implied volatility, you can estimate the price range of the stock. That can be done using a simple formula.

(Stock price x implied volatility)/SQRT (days in a year)

If you don't want to do the calculation, if we take the square root of 365, it is about 19.1. For example, we use Facebook with a share price of $202.50 and implied volatility of 76%.

The implied volatility gives us an idea of what traders are thinking regarding the upcoming earnings call. Still, of course, we can never be sure what is going to happen until it does. But this gives us upper and lower bounds. Using the information that we have available; we can guess that Facebook might rise to $210.56 a share after the earnings call. It might drop to $194.44 per share after the earnings call. You can use these boundaries to set up your strategy. However, remember that if there is a big surprise, it can go well past these boundary points in one direction or the other.

What is a Long Straddle?

To set up a straddle, you buy a put option and a call option simultaneously (buy = take a long position). The maximum loss that you can incur is the sum of the cost to buy the call option plus the amount of the damage to buy the put option. This loss is incurred when you enter the trade.

With a straddle, you buy a call option and a put option together. And they would be with the same strike price. By necessity, this means that one option will be in the money, and one option will be out of the money. When approaching an earnings call, the prices can be kind of steep, because you want to price them close to the current share price. That way, it gives us some room to profit either way the stock price moves.

A maximum loss is only incurred if you hold the position to expiration. You can always choose to sell it early if it looks like it's not going to work out and take a loss that is less than the maximum.

There is a total premium paid for entering into the position. This is the amount of cash paid for buying the call added to the money paid for buying the put. This is called the total premium. There are two breakeven points:

To the upside, the breakeven point is the strike price + total premium paid.

On the downside, the breakeven point is the strike price – total premium paid.

It the price of the stock moves up past the breakeven point, the put is worthless. However, the call option would earn substantial profits. On the other hand, if the stock price moved down past the lower price point, that would be the breakeven, the call option would be worthless, and the put option would earn substantial profits.

For example, suppose that we buy a $207.5 straddle on Apple 7 days to expiration with an implied volatility of 35%. The underlying price is $207. The total cost to enter the position is $8.03 ($803 total). At one day to expiration, the share price breaks up to $220 a share after the earnings call. The put expires worthless, but the call jumps to $12.50. The net profit is then $12.50 - $8.03 = $4.47, or $447 in total per contract.

If instead, the share price had dropped to $190, the call expires worthless, and the put jumps to $17.50 per share. The net profit, in this case, is then $17.50 - $8.03 = $9.47 per share or a total of $947.

This isn't to say that the straddle would be more profitable for a stock decrease; it is not. The profit will be the same no matter which way the share price moves; in our examples, we used two different sized steps. The point is to illustrate that nothing in which direction the stock moves, you can profit.

If the stock is at the money at expiration, we could still recoup some of the investment and sell the straddle for a loss. In this case, the call and the put would both be priced at $152. We'd still be at a loss, but we could recoup $304 by selling both at $152.

Short Straddle

If you sell a straddle, then you are taking the opposite position, which means you would be betting that the share price stays inside the range and hope that the stock didn't make a big move to the upside or the downside. To sell a straddle, you'd have to either be able to do a covered call and protected put or be a level 4 trader who could trade naked options.

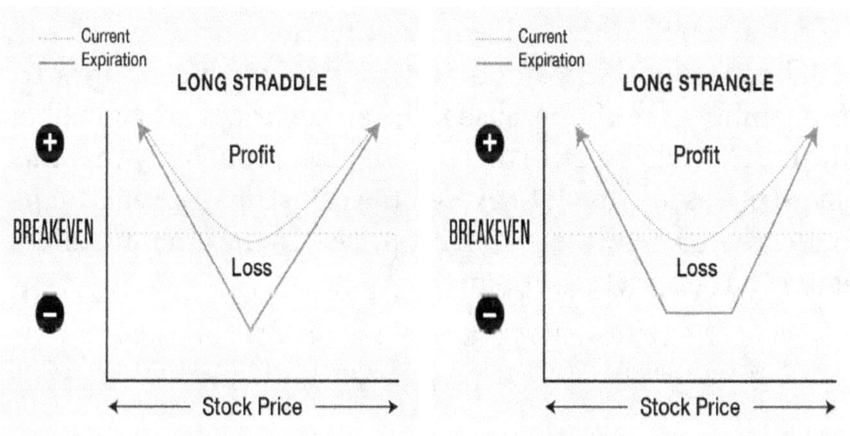

Long Strangle

A strangle is similar to a straddle, but in this case, the strike prices are different. In this case, you will buy a barely out of the money call option while simultaneously purchasing a slightly out of the money put option. The two options will have the same expiration date. The breakeven points for a strangle are going to be calculated similarly as the breakeven prices for a straddle. Still, you will use the individual strike prices for the call and put that because they are different. You calculate the total premium paid, which is the total amount paid for the call option plus the premium paid for the put option. Then the breakeven points are given by the following formulas:

To the upside, the breakeven point is the strike price of the call + total premium paid.

On the downside, the breakeven point is the strike price of the put – total premium paid.

Similarly, compared to a long straddle, the maximum loss is going to occur when the share price ends in between the two strike prices. Therefore, you might want to choose relatively close strike prices to minimize the range over which the loss can occur. Of course, there is a trade-off here because the closer in the field the strike prices are, the more expensive it will be to enter the position. But, it's going to increase your probability of profit because if the strike prices are tight about the current share price, there is a higher probability that the share prices are going to exceed the call strike + premium paid, or decrease below the put strike price less the amount paid to enter the contract (the bonus).

Chapter 8: LEAPS

LEAPS (Long-term equity anticipation securities) step away from the norm and have a longer shelf-life compared to your average option. They still possess the qualities as a reasonable option. LEAPS appeal to investors that want a long-term investment without being obliged by that investment. It also appeals to the investor who is anticipating a profitable yield from a particular market in the future but does not have the capital to make that substantial investment. They are more affordable than such assets like the stock because, despite the more extended expiration date, they are still options and, thus, stick to option price ranges. LEAPS typically have a slightly higher price than other short-term contracts

LEAPS have a seat at the options table because sometimes the value of the associated asset needs more time to appreciate. Typical options expire in a few months. These options can yield profits in a short amount of time. Still, there is also the risk that the transaction might not be as profitable if the stock or other associated asset does not move significantly up or down.

LEAPS are the solution that allows that time for appreciation of the associated asset. A trader can even extend the expiration on that LEAP option with another LEAP if the period is still too short for the asset to reach profitability. For example, a LEAP with an expiration date of 2 years can be held for one year then be sold to replace it with a 3-year expiration date. This is called rolled LEAPS.

Rolling the option forward usually is relatively inexpensive because it still carries the same characteristics. Other factors can become unpredictable, though. Such factors include interest rates, dividends, and volatility.

The question that stumps many traders about LEAPS is whether to use a call option or a put option. The answer to that is dependent on whether the trader expects a bullish or bearish price movement. If the trader believes that the associated asset is bullish by the expiration date, he or she should buy call options. If instead he or she understands that the related asset will drop in value by the expiration date, then the trader should buy put options.

Best Strategies for Using LEAPs

Some strategies work best when it pertains to LEAPS, and this list includes:

- Long call. This involves the purchase of LEAPS call options in anticipation of a long-term bullish trend in the market.

- Long put. This involves the purchase of LEAPS put options in anticipation of a long-term bearish trend in the market.

- Rolling LEAPS options. As mentioned earlier, this involves selling the LEAPS before expiration date while buying LEAPS with similar characteristics with at least 2-year expiration dates at the same time.

- Bull call spread. This options strategy is considered to reduce the initial cost of buying a call option. This can help offset the higher cost of LEAPS compared to standard options. Only use this strategy if you are confident that there will be a moderate rise in the stock price to send it up to the strike price.

- Bull call spread. This is another strategy meant to

offset the higher cost of LEAPs. It is a bearish strategy. Profits are earned when the stock prices fall.

- Calendar call spread. This strategy is meant for a trader who wishes to benefit from the associated assets staying stagnant in the market while also helping from the long-term call position if it becomes more valuable in the future.

The Benefits of LEAPS

LEAPS have several benefits, and they include:

- LEAPS are sustainable as they allow a trader to piggyback off-market trends. This allows the trader to observe the movement of stock prices and have an option to buy or sell without making the full commitment of ownership.

- LEAPS is less volatility, and so offers greater security. A trader who enters into such an option is looking at a stock increasing or decreasing in price over the long haul. This allows the trader the time to ponder on the profitability of pursuing the asset. This person can use data offered over that time, such as the current trends, news, and terms to base their future decision.

- LEAPS can serve considerable security in your financial portfolio and provide shareholders with a more excellent grip on the stock.

- LEAPS allow time for improvisation because the expiration date is longer.

- Buying LEAPS is cheaper than repurchasing several standard options to back.

The Disadvantages of LEAPS

There are two sides to every coin. So, just as LEAPS are beneficial, there are also a few downsides. The first disadvantage of LEAPS is the strike price. Because they are priced higher, the trader needs to see movement in the asset price to gain a profit and take longer for the option holder to breakeven.

The longer expiration dates on LEAPS make them less predictable. Therefore, pricing correctly so that a return is seen without the transaction being too costly is made can be difficult. Lastly, the trader will not benefit from any attached dividends or stock repurchase.

LEAPS are also sensitive to implied volatility and so, can lower in value when suggested volatility drops.

Tips for Getting the Most Out Of LEAPS

- Pretend as if you are investing. This allows you to search for assets that you are interested in and maybe already have some know-how. This makes it a lot easier to keep up-to-date with market trends than if you do not know anything about the asset and are not interested in learning more.

- Make use of the extended expiration date. The benefits of the long expiration date have been stated, so ensure that these work to your advantage.

- Choose LEAPS that are more liquid.

- Prepare for the fact that LEAPS are more volatile than

stocks but less volatile than standard options.

- Set targets for the stock prices in comparison to your LEAPS. Knowing those targets will allow the trader to sell at the most profitable time.

- Have an exit strategy in case the option is not working out according to plan.

- Always be aware of your position and be prepared to leverage it. Even though the expiration date is far off, you need to keep abreast of whether the market is playing out as you anticipated. You need to be aware of the fluctuations in the asset's price. This will allow you to decide that makes this transaction the most profitable it can be for you. You can implement strategies like rolling the option forward and selling the first option as a loss to move to another strike price that benefits you more.

LEAPS stand for Long-term Equity Anticipation Securities. LEAPS is an excellent option for a long-term investor who wants to experiment with possibilities without being apprehensive about the volatility of the financial market in the short term. LEAPS are also an excellent way for investors who do not have an enormous amount of capital available to them at present to enter into the market with lowered risk.

This long-term maturity does have many benefits, such as being sustainable, more secure, and not subject to the decay of time. However, there are disadvantages as well, like the option being higher priced than standard options, being less predictable because of the far-off timeline, and taking longer to breakeven compared to a standard option.

To get the most out of trading LEAPS, the trader needs to be strategic. Tips like staying abreast of market trends despite having a more extended expiration date, having an exit plan if things go left field, and being prepared to leverage your position will help the trader gain maximum profit.

Chapter 9: The Greeks

Now that we know what drives option prices, we should make it more quantifiable. That signifies done using the so-called "Greeks", five parameters denoted by Greek letters, which quantify how an option's price will change. You don't need to know how they work precisely, but you have to understand what they mean when deciding on a trade genuinely. You can look up to them at any given time to get their values.

If you look at the data for any option, you will see five Greek letters (usually represented by their English spelled names

Delta	Gamma	Theta	Vega	Rho
Δ	Γ	Θ	ν	ρ

Delta, Theta, Gamma, Vega, and Rho).

Delta

The first is Delta, which shows how the price of an option varies with the underlying stock price.

We stated earlier that there is no 1-1 shift concerning the stock price and option price. By looking at Delta, you will see just how it would change.

For simplicity, we will start discussing a Call Option.

If a Call has a 0.46 delta, if the underlying stock price goes up by $1, the call option price will go up by $0.46.

Put options have a negative delta, which means that a put option has an inverse relation to the underlying stock price. That is, if the underlying stock's price falls, the value of a put option rises, and if the underlying stock's price goes up, the value of the put option falls.

Therefore, if Delta is -0.26, and the underlying stock price goes up by $1, the put option's value would decline by 26 cents. On the other hand, if the underlying stock price had fallen by $1, the put option price would go up by $0.26.

For simplicity, let's consider the relationships above to be valid to grasp the core of the matter. However, keep in mind that the connection is not reliable because other factors affect the options price.

Delta is dynamic, and when any significant parameter changes in the options price, the Delta will change too.

Another thing that happens is that the closer you get to expiration; the higher Delta goes when the option remains retained. For our example of a $100 share price option, if the underlying stock price stays at $103, moving from expiry to 7 days, delta leaps for the call to 0.92. Moving to the expiry of 3 days, the Delta is 0.98.

Therefore, if you expect a stock price to change a lot in the next few days, it could be a worthwhile investment to get an option that will expire shortly before the move happens. Look for events that might influence the price, such as a call to earnings or an announcement of a purchase.

Note that "at the money" options have a delta of approximately 0.50. When you get close to maturity, the Delta for a call will be exactly 0.50, and for a put, it will be -0.5.

If an option is out of the money, you get the smaller Delta getting closer to the expiration date. In reality, it can become vanishingly small a few days away from the expiry delta.

For example, a $100 strike price Call option, on a $97 share price with three days to expire, would have a 0.02 delta.

The Delta should also sum up the difference to 100 for the same put option (but note it does express as a negative value).

So, in the example above, a put option with the same conditions would have a delta of -0.98. To consider a real case scenario, these puts would be worth $3.00 in that situation. If the underlying share price fell to $96, the put price would increase to $4. You will then see the Delta rise to -1.00 for a put, and decrease to 0.00 for a call.

If the stock went the other way, the price increased by $1, then the Delta for the put would drop to -0.92, and the put price would drop to $2.04.

You can allegedly expect this kind of option premiums movements on the market.

The bottom line is Delta should give you a fair approximation of how much the option price should change if the underlying stock price increases by $1. If this is a call option, the relationship is direct, and the Delta remains expressed as a positive number. For put options, because the link is the opposite, the Delta is a negative number.

Gamma

Gamma is a derivative of the Delta. It shows you how the Delta changes itself. That is significant as we found the Delta was dynamic.

Beginner traders don't need to delve too deeply into this. You can test Gamma to see how much Delta can change if the price of the underlying shares increases by $1. For both puts and calls, Gamma has the same value. And if Gamma were 0.22

and Delta was 0.24 for a Call Option, and -0.76 for a Put Option of the same strike and expiration date, we would expect a $1 rise in share price trigger a Delta raise for the call option to 0.46. The put option delta will adjust to -0.54.

Theta

Theta is a very significant parameter among the Greeks when analyzing options. Theta gives you details about the option's time decay. Theta is a negative number, representing that time decay, as time goes on, always causes a decline in the price of options. Let's take in a few examples.

Suppose we have a call and put options at a $100 strike price with three days to expire. The call price is $1.20, and the put price is $0.20 if the underlying stock price is $101. In this case, for both the call and the put theta is -0.073. That tells us that if nothing else changes, each option's price will go down $0.073. Moving to 2 days before expiration and leaving all else the same, we see the call option price falling to $1.12. The put option price is dropping to $0.12, so it moved almost precisely to what planned. The next day theta has fallen to -0.079, reflecting that time decay happens quicker, the closer you get to the option's expiry date.

Twenty days to the expiration, Theta, with everything else unchanged, was about half as high, at -0.035.

That represents one of the essential truths of options; that is, time decay occurs exponentially, with time decay occurring faster the closer you get to expiration.

One of the factors that can make solutions appear confusing is the interdependence of all of these variables. So, imagine the stock price shot up to $108 at 20 days to expiry. In that case, Theta would have been -0.005, which is just 1/7th of the previous value.

Likewise, Theta is proportional to the share price. And if the share price is higher, the Theta is smaller. Consider a stock that has a $975 share price, and a $1,000 strike price.

The fundamental lesson here is the same as before. When it comes to pricing options, time decay is an important fundamental one.

Vega

The next Greek we will encounter is Vega, which tells us the relation between the option price and the implied volatility. Generally speaking, an option in the money is less sensitive to changes in implied volatility. In contrast, a choice out of the money is more sensitive to changes in implied volatility. In particular, Vega informs you how much the option price would change if the suggested volatility changes by 1 percent. Remember, options with higher mean implied volatility are worth more money.

 Let's consider a stock currently traded at $500 a share. A strike price of $490 with ten days left to expire and an associated 23.5 percent volatility. Vega is 0.3.

A call would remain valued at $13.7, and a put would be assessed $3.7 with the same parameters.

If the volatility implied increase to 24.5 percent, the call would remain priced at $14, and the put would be $4.

In other words, Vega tells you how much the price of the options increases for every percentage point increase in implied volatility. The closer you get to the expiration date, the smaller the Vega will be.

Rho

Rho is a calculation of the resilience of option price against a risk-free interest rate adjustment. Since interest rates these days don't change by that much or that often, rho isn't given much attention. Rho will be a more significant parameter to pay attention to in a dramatically evolving high-interest-rate setting, such as in the late 1970s.

Equation of Black-Scholes:

As we already assessed, the comparison of Black-Scholes is a partial differential equation that predicts a European option's future price according to the Black-Scholes mathematical model. The option price continues evaluated as a function of the underlying stock price, time, portfolio volatility, and risk-free interest rate.

In economics, the model has contributed to a Nobel Laureate. One crucial fact is that the model designed to work with European options that can only use at the expiry date and that it does not work with American options. However, for American options, several other mathematical models function very well.

However, most options traders do not care about the Black-Scholes equation.

You can simply use tools such as spreadsheets or online models that people have developed to bring the equation into action. You can play with the various inputs to predict the possible price movements of options in which you are involved.

Minor Greeks

Other less critical Greeks influence an option price but in a minor way. These are the second or third partial derivatives of the major ones and have a secondary effect on the option price.

Namely, they are Lambda, Epsilon, Vomma, Vera, Speed, Zomma, Color, and Ultima.

Their use has seen a boost in the latest years due to the increasing computational capacity of the PCs. The software can easily take them into account when estimating a future option price.

Summary

- You will see five Greek letters (usually represented by their English spelled names) Delta, Theta, Gamma, Vega, and Rho if you look at the data for any option.

- Delta shows you how the price of an option varies with the underlying stock price.

- Gamma is a derivative of the Delta, and it shows you how the Delta changes itself. That is significant as we found the Delta was dynamic

- Theta is a substantial parameter among the Greeks when analyzing options. Theta gives you details about the option's time decay.

- Vega tells us the relation between the option price and the volatility implied.

- Rho is a calculation of the resilience of pricing options against a risk-free interest rate adjustment

Chapter 10: Debit and Credit Spreads

Debit

A debit spread is the purchase of one option and the sale of another option of the same type and with the same expiration date with different strike prices, such that the complete transaction results in a net debit. There are two types of debit spreads. You can do a call debit spread, which means buying a call and selling a call, or you can do a put debit spread, which means buying a put and selling a put simultaneously. The purpose of a debit spread is to reduce the amount of risk you face if the trade does not work, but this comes at the expense of capping profits below what you would get with an equivalent winning trade just buying a call or a put.

Let's consider the situation involving calls first. A call debit spread is also known as a bull debit spread or a bull call spread. The reason for the terminology is that this is a trade that you would enter into if you were bullish on the stock. In other words, you're expecting the stock's share price to increase by the time the options expire.

This is a two-legged trade, meaning that we are going to trade two options simultaneously. The two options will have different strike prices, but the same expiration dates. This makes the trade a vertical spread, the vertical being along with the strike prices. For a call debit spread, you will buy a call option with a lower strike price and sell an out of the money call option with a higher strike price.

Entering into this type of spread is going to change the Greeks associated with a position compared to only buying a call option at a given strike price. It will reduce the delta and theta for the trade. This means that with a smaller delta, your position will be impacted less by changes in the underlying stock price. But that isn't a concern. There is still enough delta that trade can be profitable. Our position is also less sensitive to theta, which means it will be a little less sensitive to time decay as far as losing value. But don't rest on your laurels, any option position that you enter with net debt (aka buying to enter the position) is impacted by time decay, and a call debit spread is no exception.

To make a profit, we need the underlying stock price to appreciate. The maximum profit that you can earn on a call debit spread is as follows:

Max profit = difference in strike prices – premium paid to enter the position

Looking at Apple, here are a couple of examples. We could enter into a call debit spread using two out of the money options by buying the $302.50 strike price and selling the $307.50 strike price. The cost to enter this position with one week to expiration is $1.19. The width of the strike prices is:

$307.50 - $302.50 = $5

Therefore, the maximum profit is found by subtracting the cost to enter the position from this value:

$5 - $1.19 = $3.81

Once again, there are 100 underlying shares, so it would cost $119 to enter the position, and we could earn $381. Again, this is a capped amount. Maximum profit occurs if the share price goes above the strike price of the call option that we sell (the short call) to enter the position. If you had only bought a put option, your possible profits could be much higher. No matter how much higher the stock price goes above the strike price of the short option, your profit stays the same at a fixed amount. Any time you enter into a call debit spread, if the share price of the underlying stock goes above the short strike price, sell the position to get out of it with your profits. If conditions warrant it, you can just let the options expire.

Maximum losses for a call debit spread are capped. The maximum loss that you can incur with a call debit spread is when the underlying stock price drops below the high strike price (that is the strike price of the option that you buy to enter into the position). Again, this is a fixed value. So, no matter how low the price of the underlying stock drops, even if it were to drop to zero, the number of losses that you could incur would be limited to the premium paid to enter the position.

The breakeven point occurs at the strike price of the long call plus the premium paid to enter the position. Using the Apple example, the premium paid was $1.19, and the lower strike price (or the strike price of the long call) was $302.50. So, the breakeven point is $302.50 + $1.19 = $303.69. Let's summarize this for our example, and this will help you understand how these trades work:

- If the stock drops below $302.50, we incur the maximum loss even by a penny. That is the premium paid to enter the position, which would be $1.19 per share or $119 for the 100 shares in total.

- The breakeven point is $302.50 + $1.19 = $303.69. If the stock is between $302.50 and $303.69, we incur losses, but they will be less than the total premium paid. If it reaches $303.69, we neither lose nor earn money.

- In between $303.69 and the short strike price of $307.50, we would earn a small profit.

- If the underlying share price were to go above $307.50, we'd earn a maximum profit of $381. Even if the share price were to go up to $500, it wouldn't matter, our profit is strictly capped in this trade.

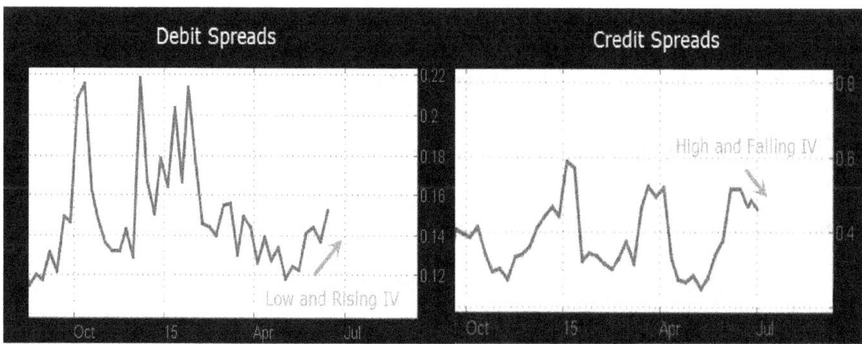

A call debit spread is a smarter way to play rising stock prices than buying call options. You cut your risk because when you sell a call option, you get paid premium for that call option. Since the strike price is higher than the strike price for the long call in this trade, the amount you get paid is lower than the amount spent to buy the long call. However, it reduces the amount you have to pay compared to buying the long call by itself.

Credit

Now let's continue our investigation of vertical spreads but shift gears. This time, we will talk about using options to generate income, rather than speculating on the direction of the stock. Of course, there is always a little bit of speculation, but in this case, we are only hoping that the price stays above a specific value, and not worry about what it is doing otherwise.

A put credit spread is created by trading two put options simultaneously. It can be said that this is set up just like the put debit spread, but we reverse the roles of which option is bought or sold. In this case, we are going to sell a put option with a higher strike price. The purpose of doing so is to generate a credit to our account that earns income. To reduce our overall risk of the trade, we will sell a put option with a lower strike price. A put option with a higher strike price will cost more than a put option with a lower strike price; therefore, there is a net credit on the trade.

There is only one rule to use when deciding to trade put credit spreads. You want to trade put credit spreads in good markets. It doesn't have to be a particularly strong bull market; it just has to be a market where prices are not declining. This applies to the individual stock as well, so you want to trade put credit spreads when the stock is doing well. A good rule of thumb is to avoid trading put credit spreads during the week of an earnings call when stock prices might suddenly plummet.

The main thing to learn about put credit spreads is that this is a selling position. You are going to sell to open, and therefore you will have the obligations of a seller associated with the short put with the higher strike price. That is, you could be "assigned." When a put option is exercised, the buyer will sell you 100 shares of stock at the strike price, no matter the market price. And theoretically, you need to have the cash on hand to cover the transaction. When you are assigned, you are required by law to buy the 100 shares.

But the good news about the put credit spread is you don't have to buy the shares, and your liability is capped. The reason is that you have covered yourself by purchasing a put option with a lower strike price. What happens is you can exercise the put option with the lower strike price. It works like this – you have to buy the 100 shares at the higher strike price. But you can turn around and sell them at the lower strike price by exercising the other put option. With a credit spread, you are assigned one option and can exercise the other option. You would lose money in this situation; the difference between the strike prices minus the net credit received. But at least it is a fixed amount of money.

In practice, you aren't going to have to do anything at all, because your broker takes care of all this automatically in the event the option expires in a situation where it could be exercised. As a trader, you won't know all this happened, the stocks will be bought and sold on your behalf, and you will only see the result.

To sell put options, you are going to need some collateral. This is done by putting a cash deposit into your account. The purpose of doing so is to cover the theoretical loss that can occur if the trade does not work out for you. To see how this works, let's look at an example.

Consider a put credit spread on Apple that expires in one week. The strike prices are $297.50 and $295. The breakeven price is the strike price of the short put option, $297.50, less the net credit received. Remembering that with a credit spread, you don't pay anything to enter the position. You are receiving credit for it. But you won't see the credit materialize until the options expire or you repurchase it.

In this case, the credit received is $1.12 per share, or $100. So, the breakeven point is $296.38. As long as the stock price stays above $296.38, you will make a profit (at the time of writing, it's $297.35). Maximum gain happens if the stock price stays or goes above the upper strike price. So, if it stays at or goes above $297.50 per share, a real possibility in this case, then you would earn the maximum credit of $112. Maximum loss is computed by taking the difference between the strike prices and subtracting the credit received. In this case, we have ($297.50 - $295) - $1.12 = $1.38, or $138.

To enter the trade, you would have to deposit some cash to cover that potential loss.

Chapter 11: Common Mistakes and How to Avoid Them

We learn from our mistakes. There is no better teacher in life than experience. But what if we don't have to make mistakes because we have learned from the mistakes of others? Isn't that better? This is why we are going to discuss common mistakes traders, especially beginners, make during trading, and how to avoid them. We know that learning from your practice sticks more, but let this guide be your chaperone; that little voice in your head telling you what not to do. We tagged them "The Ten Commandments for Successful Trading." So, you shall:

1. Have a trading plan

2. Not buy cheap options

3. Not get carried away by the leverage of options

4. Not play too safe

5. Not fail to close the trade before expiration

6. Belong to a community

7. Not trade low volume options

8. Not cut your losses by doubling up

9. Have an exit plan

10. Not believe that the more complex strategy yields more reward

No trading plan

Every productive venture in life begins with a plan. From

building houses to going to school to starting a relationship to starting a business. It all starts with a plan. Defining where to start, what to do when you start, and where to end. Amateur traders often make the mistake of thinking the trading options is just a hobby, a game. The charts are fascinating. The red and green candlesticks are attractive to the computer. But those candlesticks represent the condition of your investment. Therefore, it is essential to treat your trades as a business. And a company starts with a business plan. Your plan should define how much you are willing to risk, the strategy you would adopt, and your exit strategy. We will discuss extensively on how to build a trading plan.

Buying cheap options

Many traders begin trading by buying OTM options with short expiration dates because they are cheap. The plan is to spend less to gain more. They forget that they do not control the market. As the expiration date draws closer, the probability of the option getting in-the-money becomes slimmer. Most times, for that to happen, traders have to bank on a robust fundamental analysis — which may or may not occur. Traders who purchase cheap options are attracted by the low premiums that they forget to guide their predictions with accurate reports. They are taking a gamble. One which they may likely lose.

It is better to purchase ATM or ITM options. True, they may be more expensive, but you stand a higher chance of making profits from such possibilities.

Getting carried away by the leverage of options

What makes options so attractive is the multiplier or leverage effect. Beginning traders are more focused on the enormous profits that can be made that they forget one crucial life's principle: the bigger the reward, the bigger the risk. If the trade swings to your favor, you gain the same or even higher profits than another trader who holds a similar position in the stock market. However, if the trade goes awry, your loss is more substantial because buying options include paying premiums and other commissions. The risks in options trading are even more significant when you are writing options, especially call prospects. If the printed option doesn't expire worthlessly, you would have to buy the stock at a higher price and sell at the buyer's strike price. And sometimes, the premium received for the option can't mitigate such a loss.

To hold a small position as a beginner. Do not buy or sell multiple options contracts because you are gunning for huge profits. It is better to make consistent, small profits than risk making a huge profit at once, then end up losing your entire investment.

Playing too safe

Many beginners are so scared of losing their investments that they only purchase long calls and long puts. While it is good to be reliable, such a practice will be detrimental to your trading experience because you won't grow as a trader. The options market is a dynamic one; that is why there are many strategies that you can use to flow with the progress of the market. There are strategies for any condition of the market — upward price movement (e.g., long call), downward price movement (e.g., long put), increased volatility (e.g., straddle), decreased volatility (e.g., calendar spread), no price movement (e.g., short condor), or time decay (e.g., iron condor).

Study the market and test these strategies with little funds. When you have mastered them, you can use them to cash out from the market, no matter which direction it goes.

Failing the close trade before expiration

This happens to emotional traders. An emotional may fail to close the business before the end because he is in profit and wants to make more — greed. Or he is at a loss and expects the price of the underlying to move dramatically so he can make a profit — fear. In the end, they probably forget to close the trade, and their entire option expires worthless since it wasn't exercised. Trading options is always a race against time, and you should not make the mistake of losing your investment just because you want more. There will always be more trades. The market is not closing, so cut your losses or take your profits instead of losing everything.

Not belonging to a community

Many traders try to trade in isolation. They do this because they are trying to protect themselves from conflicting ideas. This reason is logical because, in a booming market with many divergent views, one may tend to get confused. However, this does not downplay the importance of belonging to a community. As a trader, you need to stay informed. And there is news you would not get by trading alone. You have to interact and hear the ideas of others. You must sift the information you receive. How do you do this? If an idea is not in line with your plan, then discard it. The design may be worthwhile for another but may be risky for you. A trader may suggest an opinion because he has enough funds. He is willing to risk to try it out. It will be foolhardy to try it out too with your little funds.

To receive information and process them before using them as tools for trading. But don't make the mistake of being uninformed.

Trading low volume options

Low volume options are illiquid. There are many ways to look at liquidity. One, liquidity refers to the ability to buy or sell an underlying asset quickly without a change in price. Two, it relates to the presence of active buyers and sellers at all times, trading a particular stock or option. When there is a high presence of buyers and sellers, there is increased competition, and the bid-ask spread of the option is low. Bid-ask spread shows how much a trader is willing to buy an option and how much a trader is ready to sell an option. With illiquid options, this spread is high. Three (which is most essential for us), the liquidity of an option refers to how quickly it can be sold or converted to cash at the current market price.

This implies that writing illiquid options may not be profitable for you. This is because you may not be able to sell it, or if you do, you will sell at a discounted price below the market price or the price you were willing to sell. Usually, OTM options are more illiquid than ATM or ITM options. Also, long-term prospects are more illiquid than short-term opportunities.

Cutting losses by doubling up

This is another result of trading with your emotions. Some traders choose to double up instead of exiting a trade. By doubling up, we mean taking the same trade position even when the market flows in the opposite direction. For example, a trader purchases a call option. Before expiration, the price of the underlying steadily moves below the strike price. Instead of the trader to exit the trade, he buys another call option at a lower strike price hoping for the stock price to bounce back to an upward movement. Such practice heightens the overall risk of the investment.

As a beginner, you have to avoid this. Remember that a trader cannot control the market, but a trader can control their emotions and decisions. You should exit the trade early and move on. Go back to your plan and know what to do next time.

Not having an exit plan

Every building has exited. When writing a business plan, an exit plan is included. So, your trading plan should have a defined exit strategy. Traders make mistakes like doubling up because they don't have an exit plan. They don't know what to do when the trade goes south. Some option writers are guilty of this as well. They write an option and lean onto hope — expecting the option to expire worthlessly. But this is a terrible practice. Before writing an opportunity, make sure you have enough funds to buy back (written put) or sell (written call) the underlying if the trade doesn't go your way. You should understand that you have no control over when the buyer of the contract would choose to exercise the option. The buyer may choose to apply it before the expiration, and you are obligated to trade at the strike price. So be prepared.

Furthermore, having an exit plan is not restricted to cutting losses alone. You should also have an exit plan, even if you are in profit. Set a mark for yourself. For instance, as a trader, you can decide to take only a 10% profit. It doesn't matter to you whether the asset further increases in value. Setting such standards and keeping to them helps improve your discipline and strengthen your emotion.

Believing that more complex strategies have better rewards

As humans, we tend to take significant risks because we think significant risks yield big rewards. We are often motivated by mantras such as "No pain, no gain" or "No guts, no glory."

These mantras are correct. But we would recommend you take more significant risks if that is the only option available. There are many strategies available in the world of possibilities, and each offers unique risks and rewards. There is no point going for an iron butterfly when you can easily use a covered call. Study the market terrain and employ the best strategy suitable for the market and also your portfolio.

Stick with what works for you. Live by the two accessible rules of Warren Buffet. "Rule No.1: Never lose money. Rule No. 2: Never forget rule No.1." So, stick to the strategies you trust. Strategies that will make you profit. Only use a sophisticated approach when necessary.

You have gotten useful tips about trading intelligently, controlling your emotions, and avoiding common mistakes. The next question is, where do you apply these tips? What platforms can you use to trade options? What tools are available for you?

Properly Allocate Funds to Trades

You should allocate funds correctly to your trades. You do not want to allocate any amount above 5% of your investments to a single business. Choose several deals and allocate each trade an amount between 3% and 5%. This way, you will stand to win a lot more than lose. You will also spread your risk and avoid losing all your money.

Chapter 12: Choosing A Broker

Often, in this text, a reference was made to professional advice and guidance before and during any trading with options. In a few cases, it was also suggested that this advice and guidance were to be rendered by experts and not just professionals. But who are these people?

They are called options brokers, and their profession is to offer actual options trading, along with research, education, and various tools to individual investors. Apart from the above, they can also provide a trade-in other financial product related to options, like stocks, funds (either mutual or exchange-traded), and bonds.

As in any profession, some good brokers and brokers do not have your best interest in their minds. Here are the things to look for to select a good options broker.

First of all, you need to know if you want to deal with a regular broker or a reseller broker. The first one deals directly with you, while the latter intermediates between you and a larger broker.

Regular brokers have a better reputation than resellers. Especially those that are members of recognized organizations like F.IN.R.A. (Financial Industry Regulatory Authority) or S.I.P.C. (Securities Investor Protection Corporation). Therefore, if you choose a regular broker, the first thing to check is whether they belong to such an entity. If not, it would be best to avoid them.

The next choice to make is between a full-service broker and a discount broker. The full-service ones offer a lot more services, but they do not come cheap. They undertake a more significant part of the work to be done. They will provide the professional advice and guidance required.

On the other hand, a discount broker may be the best choice for a beginner. For two reasons: a) The fees of a full-service one are probably not affordable for a newcomer and b) You will learn a lot more about options trading if you do what has required yourself Regardless of the above, what usually affects the decisions on which broker to choose, are the costs involved. The following will weigh a lot on your selection:

Minimum balances

To start a brokerage account, most brokers require a minimum balance. This amount ranges between $500 and $1,000.

Margin accounts

While it is not an immediate choice for beginners, it will be a significant issue as you continue trading. Margin accounts are created when the broker will lend you the money to make the trades. The securities and options that you will purchase, along with the balance of your account, are held as collateral.

While it is risky (you stand to file for bankruptcy if you fail grossly), it is a handy tool to check your broker's integrity. A good broker will protest if your choices are not sound ones, and will not lend you the money as they do not want to lose it.

Easiness of withdrawal

 Just like any other professionals, brokers want to make a profit. Therefore, most of them will charge you a withdrawal fee, or will not let you close your account if the balance drops below the minimum. It is strongly recommended to make sure that you fully understand the rules about money withdrawal before you begin any cooperation with a broker.

Fee structures

Hidden fees and expenses are the greatest fear of investors. While most brokers follow similar rules, some of them have particularly complex fee structures. A general rule of thumb is that if the fees look too good to be true, make sure that you read the small print. Generally, the less complicated the fee structure is, the better the broker.

Brokers are significant, as you will not be able to start investing without a brokerage account. You should always keep in mind that no broker can be good at everything. So, the last issue to consider before selecting a broker, is what kind of investor you are. Your broker must match with your style.

Identifying a Reliable Broker
There are plenty of brokerage firms available online. These brokerage firms provide traders like you with a platform to trade safely. These firms charge you a fee to access the platform and carry out your trades. They also provide you with tools that you need to purchase successfully and customer service.

Generally, the lower the fees or commission charged, the less the customer service and assistance you can expect. On average, you should expect to pay between $2 and $5 per options contract that you invest in.

Sometimes you will be asked if you prefer a cash or margin account when opening an account with a broker. A cash account means you will trade using your own money. On the other hand, a margin account allows you access to credit facilities where you borrow money from the broker to invest in individual securities. Keep in mind that you can only borrow money from your broker against particular securities like bonds, stocks, and mutual funds.

You will not be able to borrow to invest in stock options because they are strictly cash-only trades. Options also settle trades the very same day or one business day. Therefore, you will require substantial cash amounts to enter trades. When you enter complex deals, you will also need to set some cash aside just if you are obliged to buy shares at a specific price.

When opening an account, ensure that you choose a broker that rates you:

At this level, you can trade-in options even as a beginner. Also, tick on the margin box rather than cash just so that you always have access to borrowing from the broker. There are generally four levels of traders. They range from level 0 to level 3.

At level 3, you are allowed to enter profitable but risky trades. For instance, you can participate in naked calls and naked puts. You can also engage in other, more complicated trades. However, risky businesses will require much higher deposits, so keep this in mind. All in all, brokers are all different. However, they will all need you to have access to cash and stocks in your account. This way, you will be able to fulfill your obligations and trade as often as you need. Therefore, you will access options markets via your broker. Your broker will usually have access to the major platforms where options are traded.

Are you enjoying this book? I would be very grateful if you let me know your opinion with a short review on Amazon. Thank you.

Chapter 13: Options Trading and the Individual Investor

This chapter looks at the setups for profitable trades - to get a rough overview and see where the market is in general development. Then we turn to the technical tools to find an entry point, stop-fall protection, if you're wrong, and the likely candidates for the price moves. As in the real estate business, trading is the essential factor: the location, the location, the location. Then there is the timing, the timing, the timing. The setup gives you a rough overview of the market's current state of development - essential when looking for short-term reversal or confirmation patterns. Ideally, you open your position in the area where the likelihood of success is most magnificent.

How Does the Stock Market Work?

A Stock market analysis looks like gibberish to beginners and average investors. However, you should know that the way this market works is quite simple. Just imagine a typical auction house or an online auction website. This market works in the same way - it allows buyers and sellers to negotiate prices and carry out successful trades. The first stock market took place in a physical marketplace. However, these days, deals happen electronically via the internet and online stockbrokers. From the comfort of your homes, you can quickly bid and negotiate for stock prices with online stockbrokers.

Furthermore, you might come across news headlines that say the stock market has crashed or gone up. Once again, don't fret or get all excited when you come across such news. Most often than not, this means a stock market index has gone up or down. In other words, the stocks in a market index have gone down. Before we proceed, let's explore the meaning of market indexes.

Stock Market Indexes

As mentioned earlier, when people refer to the rise and fall of the stock market, they are generally referring to one of the primary stock market's market indexes. Market indexes track a group of stocks in a particular sector, like manufacturing or technology. The value of the shares featured in an index is representative of all the stocks in that sector. It is essential to take note of what stocks each market index represents. You should invest in a niche you are comfortable with. In addition to this, giant market indexes like the Dow Jones Industrial Average, the NASDAQ composite, and the Standard & Poor's 500 are often used as proxies for the stock market's performance as a whole. You can choose to invest in an entire index through the exchange-traded funds and index funds, as it can track a specific sector or index of the stock market.

Bullish and Bearish Markets

Talking about the optimistic outlook of the stock market is guaranteed to get beginners looking astonished. Yes, it sounds ridiculous at first, but with time, you get to appreciate the ingenuity of these descriptions. Let's start with the bearish market. A bear is an animal you would never want to meet on a hike; it strikes fear into your heart, and that's the effect you will get from a bearish market. A bear market depicts when stock prices are falling across several of the indexes mentioned earlier. The threshold for a bearish market varies within a 20 percent loss or more.

Most young investors unfamiliar with a bear market as we've been in a bull market since the first quarter of 2019. This makes it the second-longest bull market in history. Just as you have probably guessed by now, a bull market indicates that stock prices are rising. You should know that the market is continually changing from bull to bear and vice versa. From the Great Recession to the global market crash, these changing market prices indicate the start of larger economic patterns. For instance, a bull market shows investors are investing heavily and that the economy is exceptionally well.

On the other hand, a bear market shows investors are scared and pulling back, with the economy on the brink of collapsing. If this made you paranoid about the next bear market, don't fret. Business analysts have shown that the average bull market generally outlasts the average bear market by a large margin. This is why you can grow your money in stocks over an extended period.

Stock Market Corrections and Crash

A stock market crash is every investor's nightmare. It is usually complicated to watch stocks that you've spent so many years accumulating diminish before your very eyes. Yes, this is how volatile the stock market is. Stock market crashes usually include a very sudden and sharp drop in stock prices. It might herald the beginning of a bear market. On the other hand, stock market corrections occur when the market drops by 10 percent - this is just the market's way of balancing itself. The current bull market has gone through 5 market corrections.

Analyzing the Stock Market

You are not psychic. It is nearly impossible to accurately predict the outcome of your stock to the last detail. However, you can become near perfect at reading the stock market by adequately analyzing the components of this market. There are two basic types of analyses: technical analysis and fundamental analysis.

Fundamental Market Analysis

Fundamental analysis involves getting data about a company's stocks or a particular sector in the stock market, via financial records, company assets, economic reports, and market share. Analysts and investors can conduct fundamental analysis via the metrics on a corporation's financial statement. These metrics include cash flow statements, balance sheet statements, footnotes, and income statements. Most times, you can get a company's financial statement through a 10-k report in the database. In addition to this, the SEC's EDGAR is an excellent place to get the company's financial statement. With the financial statement, you can deduce the revenues, expenses, and profits a company has made.

What's more? By looking at the financial statement, you will have a measure of a company's growth trajectory, leverage, liquidity, and solvency. Analysts utilize different ratios to make an accurate prediction about stocks. For example, the quick and current rates are useful in determining if a company will be able to pay its short-term liabilities with the existing asset. If the current ratio is less than 1, the company is in poor financial health and may not recover from its short-term debt. Here's another example: a stock analyst can use the debt ratio to measure the current level of debt taken on by the company. If the debt ratio is above 1, it means the company has more debt than assets, and it's only a matter of time before it goes under.

Technical Market Analysis

This is the second part of the stock market analysis. It revolves around studying past market actions to predict the stock price direction. Technical analysts put more focus on the price and volume of shares. Additionally, they analyze the market as a whole and study the supply and demand factors that dictate market movement. In technical analyses, charts are of inestimable value. Tables are a vital tool as they show the graphical representation of a stock's trend within a set time frame. What's more? Technical investors can identify and mark specific areas as resistance or support levels on a chart. The resistance level is a previous high stock price before the current price.

On the other hand, support levels are represented by a previous low before the current stock price. Therefore, a break below the support levels marks the beginning of a bearish trend. Alternatively, a break above the resistance level marks the beginning of a bullish market trend. Technical analysis is only useful when the rise and fall of stock prices are influenced by supply and demand forces. However, technical analysis is mostly rendered ineffective in the face of outside forces that affect stock prices such as stock splits, dividend announcements, scandals, changes in management, mergers, and so on. Investors can make use of both types of analyses to get an accurate prediction of their stock values.

Why You Need to Diversify

According to research by Ned Davis, a bear market occurs every 3.5 years and has an average lifespan of 15 months. One thing is clear, though: you can't avoid bear markets. You can, however, prevent the risks that come with investing in a single investment portfolio. Let's look at a common mistake that new investors typically make. Research points to the fact that individual stocks dwindle to a loss of 100 percent. By throwing in your lot with one company, you are exposing yourself to many setbacks. For example, you can lose your money if a corporation is embroiled in a scandal, poor leadership, and regulatory issues. So, how can you balance out your losses? By investing in the index as mentioned earlier, fund or ETF fund, as these indexes hold many different stocks, as by doing this, you've automatically diversified your investment. Here's a nugget to cherish: put 90 percent of your investment funds in an index fund, and put the remaining 10 percent in an individual stock that you trust.

When to Sell Your Stocks

One thing is sure - you are not going to hold your stocks forever. All our investment advice and energies are directed towards buying. Yes, it is the buying of stocks that kick-start the entire investment when chasing your dream concept. However, just as every beginning has an end, you will eventually sell every stock you buy. It is the natural order. Even so, selling off stock is not an easy decision. Heck! It's even harder to determine the right time to sell. This is the point where greed and human emotions start to battle with pragmatism. Many investors try to make sensible selling decisions solely based on price movements. However, this is not a sure strategy, as it is still reasonable to hold onto a stock that has fallen in value.

Conversely, selling a stock when it has reached your target is seen as prudent. So, how can you navigate around this dilemma? Before touching on other parts in this section, let's first tackle why selling is so hard.

Why Selling Is So Hard

Do you know why it's so hard to let go of your stocks even when you have a fixed strategy to follow? The answer lies in human greed. When making decisions, it's an innate human tendency to be greedy. Here's an example: An investor purchases shares at $30, and tells herself that when the stocks hit $40, she will sell. Here comes an all-too-familiar trend - when the stocks finally hit $40, the investor will hold out and see if her stock prices will rise beyond $40. You can see that human nature is already creeping in. Undoubtedly, the stocks hit $45, and greed takes over logical thinking. She decides to wait to see if it rises beyond $45. Suddenly, the stock prices plummet down to $36. At this point, she tells herself that once the stocks rise again to $40, she will sell. Unfortunately, this never happens. This stock continues to plummet down to $25. Finally, she succumbs to her frustrations and retails at $25.

Chapter 14: Methods of Buying Options and Intrinsic Time Value

Of course, choosing the right option strike price and date of expiration can be challenging. Thus, most buyers of options end up falling flat on their hands, and they end up losing their trades money.

Are you wasting money because you buy too much or not enough time?

Do you see the price of the stock shift in the direction you expected, but still lose the trade?

Look, there is an options trading learning curve, and if you have replied yes to all of these questions, that is all right. Nobody was born with a knowledge of trade options; everyone was taught to learn and to trade the markets.

For many, this means learning from errors (AKA pays your tuition on the market, in the form of commercial losses).

Furthermore, I would not be honest if I told you I had not paid my fair share of tuition in the past. But I'd like to think I graduated And I'm prepared to share a few things I've heard about purchasing options with you.

1. If you buy options, you're not just selling. Most new investors think they're going to make money if they buy a call and the stock price rises. And they're going to make money if they buy a put, and the price drops. Right! Right!

2. There are several components in which an option is priced. Notably, the stock's price movements, the selected optional price, the time to expire, and the implicated volatility. The price model choice is simply a probability model.

3. The intrinsic value and extrinsic value are options.

Example:

FACEBOOK closed on April 1, 2014, at 62.62. The average price for the 4/4/14 call (expiry) is $2.01 Intrinsic value would be actual if the option were hypothetical today.

The intrinsic value, in this case, is $1.62.

The extrinsic value is the variable time and volatility.

That is $2.01 minus $1.62 or $0.39 in this situation.

The average price for the 4/4/14 telephone call (expired) $62.5 is $1.04, the intrinsic value of $0.12, and the alien value of $0.92. As you can see, the time and uncertainty of this option are much of the interest.

Note, all options are left with their intrinsic value at expiration.

It's just another way to suggest that they either expire in cash or expire without any interest.

That will result in 88 percent of its present value losing if the stock settled at $62.62. Just three days after expiration, can you see how easily these options consume time and uncertainty?

4. Intrinsic interest is just in-the-money options. That said, money and out-of-the-money options have universal value only. The higher an option is, the more the price of the option shifts with the underlying stock.

An option in the amount can travel with the stock, but it has to overcome (accelerating) the time value. If the option volatility increases, the option can gain value, or if option volatility decreases, the option can lose value.

5. Options trading is classified almost term as "trading gamma," and further (in time) options trading are classified as "trading vega." What does that mean? What does that mean? If you pick short-term options to be acquired, you bet more in the directional change of the stock.

You not only make a bet on the stock's path if you pick more options, but you also bet the option volatility increases. (The Greek Vega option tests volatility sensitivity).

In reality, there are many mistakes here. If you buy money or money options, you need to step in a direction to solve the time decline. You need to increase the optional variance.

If you buy an option, you're still a long vega (or volatility option).

After a benefit announcement, a good example would be the Volatility option is crushed in almost all situations; often too much it overcomes the stock benefit heading in your direction, which eventually makes the option a loser.

6. When we reach maturity, the time value still accelerates. Moreover, the volatility option is a wild card. A variety of factors can drive it.

For instance:

Uncertainty-The volatility choice is often increased in biopharmaceutical companies if they have a pending announcement on product approval. The market doesn't know whether the news is good or poor. However, they fear it's going to trigger a monster-size change to the stock price.

MannKind (MNKD) is a recent example. The stock traded at about $4 per share on April 1, 2014. The $4 calls and puts, which expired on 4/4/14, cost + /- $2,40.

Following closure, their diabetes drug obtained FDA approval, and the stock price was more than 100% hours hourly. On the next day of trade, optional stability was destroyed by uncertainty.

Supply & Demand- This is typically due to different choices. For instance, Gastar Exploration Inc (GST) saw the regular 7.5x volume of options on April 1, 2014.

This demand for options triggered an enormous increase in the implied volatility of the options.

The implied volatility increased by over 21,2%.

On the other hand, as major optional sellers enter the market, the premium option decreases and implied volatility decreases.

7. The higher the implicated uncertainty, the more costly an alternative. The cheaper an option is, the lower the implied volatility is. Delta is the Greek option, which shows us how far we expect the stock price movement option to rise.

For example, if we have a 0.50 delta call option and the stock increases by $1, we can expect to make $0.50. Keep in mind that we're going to lose some time to decline capital.

We will also make money if implicit volatility increases or if implied volatility reduces, we will lose money.

Ultimately, you want to swap deltas if you are using options to make directional bets. Ideally, you would like to reduce as much as possible the time value and the volatility variable.

Intrinsic and Time Value in Options Trading
An option call is defined as "at the money" when the underlying security price and the impact price of the option are

the same or very similar. For example, let us assume that XYZ is trading at $50.00 per share, and XYZ is trading at $2.00 per contract for one month for the $50 call strike option. Please note that option premiums are per share, and each contract includes 100 shares.

The call option buyer has the right to purchase the shares at $50.00 in this case. With XYZ exchanging shares at $50.00, this right does not have an intrinsic value.

The option premium is made up of XYZ's full-time interest selling at $50.00 per share and a call strike price of 50. If the share value does not increase over one month, the time value variable decreases. The option expires without benefit.

A call option is called "out of the market" when the stock is less than the impact price. For example, a 1-month call option with a 50-strike can be exchanged at 30 cents if shares of an underlying security trading are $45.00 per share of XYZ.

By purchasing the call option, the holder of the option can acquire $50 of the underlying security. This option is called "Out of the Market" and has no intrinsic value because of the current stock trading at 45 dollars.

With the share price at $45, there is a time premium for the 50-strike contract. As with the "At the Money" option, the option expires worthless if the share value does not reach the strike price by the expiration date.

A call option is called "in cash" if the stock is higher than the strike price. When XYZ trades $55 per share, a call with a 50-stroke and one month to end call option may have a premium of $5.50. In this case, the caller is entitled to own the stock at $50.

With XYZ selling at $55 per share, the intrinsic value of the call option is 5.00. With a $50 strike and $55 XYZ tradings, it is possible to split the $5,50 premium into two components.

By extracting the strike price from the stock price, we will calculate that the option's value is 5.00. We then deduct the intrinsic value from the premium to calculate the time value of $0.50 in that case.

A place option is referred to as 'at the money' when the underlying price and the strike price of the options are equal to or similar to that.

With XYZ selling at 50 dollars a share, the pitch option may be exchanged in 50 dollars for one month. Still, with the put purchaser's right to sell at 50 dollars, since the share value is equivalent to the pitch price, there is no intrinsic value.

The 1,90 prices of the option are a time premium that ensures that if the share value is not lower than the strike price, it expires without interest.

An "Out of the Cash" option is considered when the share value of the underlying security is higher than the strike price. With XYZ trading at $55,00 per share, XYZ will trade at 25 cents for one month with a 50-dollar strike price.

In this situation, the investor can sell XYZ shares at $50, but the value of this option does not exist since the shares are already trading at $55. The share price is 55 dollars, and a 50-cent rise makes the 25-cent premium absolutely of the time value. If the share value remains higher than $50, the put option will expire without value.

A put option is described as "in the money" where the value of the underlying share is lower than the strike price. With XYZ at 45 dollars a share, a 50-stroke option can be sold at $5.40 for one month before the expiry date. The buyer has the right to sell the stock at 50.00 dollars, even though XYZ is priced at 45.00 dollars.

By extracting the share value from the strike price, we calculate the put option's intrinsic value. The 50-dollar effect minus the share value of $45 represents an intrinsic value of 5.00 The 5.40 premium can be split into two parts.

After eliminating the 5,00 intrinsic value, the option premium's time value portion can be estimated to be.40cents. When the share value remains the same, the time value portion depreciates to zero leaving only the intrinsic value.

As with the call option, if a "money put" has an intrinsic or real interest at its expiration, it will exercise automatically. Which choice to use would depend on the trader or investor's objectives. There are some advantages and disadvantages to each type of option.

An "at the money" option represents an inherent value when the underlying options start to move in the expected direction. These options are typically the most liquid, and the downside is that they are the costliest from a time value point of view.

Chapter 15: Financial Leverage

Leverage is a concept that is used by both companies and investors. For investors, the notion of leverage is used to try and increase returns that come on investment. To use leverage, you have to use various instruments, including future, options, and margin accounts.

The use of leverage n options trading helps boost your profits. Trading in options can give you enormous leverage and generate huge profits from a small investment.

Definition

Leverage is the ability to trade a large number of options using just a small amount of capital. Many traders feel that leverage is unsafe, but studies have found that the risk in leveraged options is nearly the same as non-leveraged securities.

Why Is Leverage Riskier?

Trading options using leverage is usually considered riskier because it exaggerates the potential of the business. For instance, you can use $500 to enter a trade with a potential of $7000. Remember the first rule of trading – don't trade what you cannot lose.

This isn't as true as it seems, so you must know what you are doing at all times.

Leverage makes you utilize capital more efficiently. Thus, many traders love the trade because it allows them to go for more significant positions with limited capital.

When you use leverage, you don't reduce the potential profit that you will gain; somewhat, you reduce the risk in specific trades. For instance, if you want to put your money in 10,000 options at $8 per share, you would need to risk $80,000 worth of investment. This means that the whole amount of $80,000 would be at risk. However, you can use leverage to place a smaller amount of money, thus reducing the risk of loss.

This is the way you need to look at leverage, which is the right way.

Before you can trade leverage, you need to find a way to maximize the gains in each trade. Here are a few tips that you can explore:

Know When to Run

You need to cut losses early enough and then let your winning trades run to completion. Just how you run other trades; you need to know when to cut your losses so that you don't end up bankrupt. You need to make use of stop losses when running leverage in trades.

Have a Stop Loss Set?

As a trader, you need to determine your stop-loss set so that you don't lose more than you can afford. The set that you come up with will depend upon the situation of the market at any time. Whatever the case, always make sure you have a set to guide you.

Don't Go with the Trade

Many traders try to chase a trade to the finish, which ends up discouraging them and making them lose money. Once a move happens, you need to accept and wait for the next opening. Always be patient because, just like the other opportunity came along, another one will come by.

Have Limit Orders

Instead of placing market limits, opt for limit orders instead so that you can save on fees. The limit orders also help you reign in your emotions when you trade.

Learn About Technical Analysis

Make sure you learn about technical analysis before you jump into trading. Technical analysis will make sure you have the information that you need to make decisions fast.

The Advantages of Leverage in Options Trading

When you use leverage, you increase your financial capability as a trader and enjoy better trading results. You can change the amount of leverage at your discretion. When you open a trading account, you have all the power to manage the amount of capital that you place on a trade. The good news is that you can use leverage free of charge, but you need to make sure you know how it works and whether it will work for you or not.

The level of leverage varies. Some trading platforms offer leverage from as low as 1:1 up to and beyond 1:1000. As a trader, you should go for the most considerable leverage possible to make the most significant returns.

Another advantage is that low leverage allows you as a new trader to survive. When starting in options trading, you can make small trades with little to show for your efforts. With leverage, you can make use of leverage to place trades that run into thousands of dollars without risking the same amount in terms of investment. As long as you know what you are doing, you can enjoy massive profits.

Disadvantages of Leverage in Options Trading

As much as it is an excellent way to make huge profits, you also need to understand that leverage comes with many demerits.

These include:

Magnifies the Losses

With leverage, you will be faced with huge losses if the trader decides to go the other way. And since the original outlay is way smaller than what you end up losing, many traders forget that they are placing their capital at risk. Make sure you come up with a ratio that will help protect your interests and then know how to manage trade risk.

No Privileges

When you use leverage to trade, you sacrifice full ownership of the asset. For instance, when you use leverage, you give up the opportunity of enjoying dividends. This is because the amount on the dividend is deducted from the account regardless of the trade position.

Margin Calls

A margin call is when the lender asks you to add funds to keep the trade open. You have to decide whether you wish to add funds or exit a position to reduce the exposure.

Incur Expenses

When you use leverage to trade options, you will receive the money from the lender to use the full position. Most traders opt to keep their positions open overnight, which attracts a fee to cover the costs.

How Much Leverage Do You Need in Options Trading?

Knowing how to trade options needs detailed knowledge about

the various aspects of economics. For many people, the lack of knowledge to use leverage is the primary cause of losses.

Studies show that many traders who opt for options lose money in the process. This happens whether for smaller or high leverage.

Risks of High Leverage
In options trading, the capital for placing a trade is usually sourced from a broker. While you can borrow massive amounts to place on a trade, you can gain more if it is successful.

A few years back, traders were able to offer leverages of up to 400 times the initial capital. However, rules and regulations have been, and at the moment, you can only access 50 times what you have. For instance, if you have $1000, you can control up to $50,000.

Choosing the Right Leverage
You need to look at different factors when choosing the kind of leverage that will work for you.

First, you need to start with low levels of leverage, because the more you borrow, the more you will need to pay back. Second, you need to use stops to make sure you protect the amount you have borrowed. Remember, losses won't go down well with you.

All in all, you need to choose leverage which you find is comfortable for you. If you are a beginner, go for low leverage so that you minimize risks. If you know what you are doing, then go for maximum leverage to build your returns.

Using stops on order allows you to reduce losses when the

trade changes direction. As a newbie, this is the only protection you need to make it in the market. This is because you will learn about the trades and how to place them while limiting any losses that might arise.

Chapter 16: Designing a Trading Plan

Far too many beginners set themselves up for trouble when they begin trading options by not having a plan. If you want to earn consistent profits when trading options, it is essential to have a solid trading plan and be disciplined when carrying out your trades. These days, trading options are pretty straightforward. In some ways, that is a great thing. However, it can also lead people into trouble. If you just trade options on a whim, that can end up leading to quick losses.

Options prices can move fast. A dull moment of thought illustrates what can happen. Since the price of an option could move by $50, $75, or even $90 for a mere $1 rise or decline in the price of a stock share, it's straightforward for options prices to move very quickly. These rapid and dramatic price movements can create a lot of problems for new traders. If you are only buying and selling individual call and put options, you will be very susceptible to these issues. If you were to buy five call options, and the stock price dropped by $1 with a delta of 0.75 over ten minutes, you would lose $375.

And if you get in a situation like that, you won't be sure what to do without a trading plan. Often, stock prices can quickly reverse, and a $1 rise or fall of a stock price isn't all that significant for many of the most popular stocks that have share prices that range from $100 to $2,000 per share. So, a $1 move in share price is not something necessarily unprecedented.

One of the problems with a significant drop in price is that panic may ensue, and a novice trader will sell out to cut their losses. This can turn out to be the wrong decision in many cases. So, selling options when there is a loss like that is not necessarily something that is the right decision. In this book, we will introduce the topic of technical analysis to help you learn ways to determine when to get in and out of trades. Still, the point here is that you need to have a plan in place rather than trading on emotional impulse.

This can work the other way as well. If the price of a share rises by $1, you could end up with significant gains (for example, and simplicity, assuming that you are trading call options). One of the problems that happen with novice traders is they get overwhelmed with irrational exuberance when share prices are rising. If the share price rises by $1, and you have five call options that rise in value by $345, it's easy to start having visions of making $1,000 in an afternoon. But of course, what often happens is a $1 rise in share price can suddenly turn into a $2 loss, and it can do that in a matter of minutes.

To avoid making these kinds of mistakes, it is essential to adopt trading psychology. In short, this means having a strict plan that you follow at all times. In a sense, you need to be detached from your trading on an emotional level, as if you were not the one risking the money. Of course, this is not always easy to do. If you are losing your own hard-earned money, it can be challenging to detach yourself emotionally from what's going on.

The way to do this is to set up rules ahead of time and follow them. As a part of your trading psychology, becoming organized and disciplined will be something that you need to master. If you are not the kind of person who is organized and prone to detailed planning, you will need to adjust your approach to things.

An essential part of trading psychology is not giving in to emotion. As mentioned in the introduction, you can fly into a panic when you get significant losses, and you can also become excessively happy when you get gains. When you let emotion guide your trading decisions, you will find that you make a lot of mistakes. Sometimes, luck will be involved, so traders who are prone to making emotional decisions and not carefully planning out their trades are still going to have impressive wins. This helps to keep them addicted and bring them back to make many trades. If they get a big winning trade, it will encourage them to follow the same impulsive process hoping to hit another big win.

The best trading psychology is one that begins with a long-term plan. You should sit down and figure out what your long-term goals are over different time frames. First off, you need to be thinking in terms of reasonable gains. You are not likely to build success by hoping to make a million dollars right away. Instead, think in terms of making $100 a week or $200 a week. Then map out a strategy that is going to help you realize your goals. Then once you have reached the goal, you can set a new goal to increase your income.

Trading options is not something that you can do if you have a "set it and forget it" attitude. As an options trader, although you don't necessarily have to be glued to your computer all day long, you need to be carefully tracking the movements in the share price of any underlying stock for your options. You don't want to impulsively buy an option (or ten options) and then go off and forget about them. You should be regularly checking to see how your options are doing and possibly using electronic tools to set up alerts.

Trading Journal

I believe that every options trader should keep a written record of their activities in a trading journal. Start the journal by mapping out your goals for the next three months. Include the amount of money you want to earn and develop a plan to reach your goal. Then include a record of all your trades in the journal. Include the date you enter the trade, how many options you bought or sold, and the amount of capital involved. Then when you close out your trade, update your entries with the final results. It is essential to keep a record and be honest with yourself. One of the mistakes that impulsive and emotional traders make is they don't keep a record of their actual trades. That makes it easy to fool yourself into thinking that you are breaking even or even making a profit when you are losing money.

You should also record your results, including profits and losses for each trade and any other expenses. This can be kept in written form or by using a spreadsheet. This will help you determine whether you have a winning trading program and know your actual net gain or loss. It is essential to be realistic about where you are and how well you are doing in reaching your goals. Keeping a detailed record rather than winging it is one way to do that.

If you find that you continually have losing trades, then you shouldn't keep doing what you've been doing. Obviously, in the beginning, you can expect to lose money on several of your first trades, possibly, and you might lose money on multiple trades in a row. That is fine in the first few weeks of trading. Still, if you find that after a month you are continually losing money on your trades, you will need to take a step back and do some analysis to find out why you keep losing on trades. Write down everything about the trade, including how long you stayed in the trade, what made you pick the trade, how much was invested, and so on. Are you holding on too long? Getting out too prematurely? Investing in options right before earnings calls and getting hammered by bad decisions? Getting in on a rising stock price too late, only to find that you mistimed it, and the stock price started dropping soon after you entered into your positions?

When you do your analysis and come up with some adjustments to your trading approach, you can resume trading with an updated training plan. Keep in mind that this is a work in progress, and you don't have to expect success immediately.

Be Realistic: It is not all wins.

Many traders think they are not doing well if they don't win on every trade. The reality is that even the best options traders are going to experience losses. The goal is to win more often than you lose so that you have net profits. Over time as you gain experience, you can expect to improve your performance.

Value Education

The fact that you're reading this book is a great sign! Those who are willing to study and learn will be more successful than those who simply start trading on impulse. But don't let this book be the end of your education, it should only be the beginning. There are many resources available for those who want to trade options, and you should continually take advantage of them. The more you can learn about options trading, the more likely it is that you will be successful. You should watch as many videos as you can find, learn all the different ways and strategies that can be used when trading options, and read as many books and educational materials as possible.

You should look for official information about options that can help you learn the ropes from experienced traders. Many organizations that are associated with options trading have educational materials available. I also strongly recommend that you follow the tasty trade. This is a group associated with the options trading platform Tasty Works. Still, you don't have to have an account with Tasty Works to use the educational platform. They have many educational videos that are free to view on their website and YouTube. They also have talk shows where they discuss different trading results, approaches to trading, and interviews with people who became successful options traders. Since it's free and put together by people who have been professional options traders for many decades in some cases, this is one of the best resources that you can use to educate yourself about trading options.

Use Buying and Selling Calls as a Learning Opportunity

Many novice traders have visions of making millions of dollars buying and selling individual call options. It is possible to make money trading individual calls and put options; however, very few professional traders make a career. The fact is that straight trading of individual options is not likely to bring consistent and long-term success. It is too difficult to consistently predict which way a stock price moves over short periods.

That said, everyone has to start as a level 2 trader, and you can look at the period that you spend trading call and put options as a chance to gain some experience. At first, start with single options contracts until you get used to the mentality and experience of options trading.

Chapter 17: An Example of Trade

In this chapter, we will talk about essential trading habits and give you examples of excellent option trading strategies. That way, you have a better idea of how to go about trading. Keep in mind, and this information can be used for any trading you decide to take part in. Keeping that in mind, we will dive into this chapter.

The medium and long-term investment is ideal for those who want to build capital or diversify and enhance savings over time naturally and at reduced costs. Given their versatility, ETFs can be used in different medium and long-term investment strategies. They can support or replace traditional instruments, thus allowing them to achieve the set objective. Currently, the range of ETFs is so diverse that any FCI can be replicated (at a much higher cost)

A strategy to invest its capital in the medium to long term is to resort to investment funds, whose popularity has grown progressively over the last twenty years. One of the main characteristics of the Funds is allowing the underwriter to enter the market with modest capital and obtain professional management that will allow them to obtain positive results over time, with moderate risk. Investment funds should favor more active management, even if this does not always happen. In addition to weighing on their final return, they are the highest management costs to which the same funds are subject. Their impact is felt particularly in times of slowdown or stagnation of the market. In light of this situation, the investor could find it convenient to substitute the investment in funds with that of ETFs that aim to follow the evolution of its benchmark index carefully, while offering the maximum possible transparency.

In advance, it cannot be said whether it is better to invest in funds or ETF; to make this choice, you have to decide if you want the manager to move away from the benchmark (and from which benchmark): this possibility is called "active risk." Active risk is not necessarily bad, because some managers are better than others. Still, in reality, they are few, and, not always, you can find them. If you decide to move away from the underlying risk, you must be convinced that:

good managers exist;

that they can do better than their benchmark;

above all, be able to find them!

If you think you can complete each of the three phases, it is appropriate to rely on active funds. Otherwise, ETFs are preferred because they cost less and carry precisely where you decided to go without additional surprises.

The techniques for choosing the ETF that best suits your investment strategies are different; an interesting methodology is applied to sector rotation: the market as a whole is made up of different equity sectors, corresponding to the different economic sectors and their continuous alternation from the origin to the expansion and contraction phases. Thus, the moments in which all the economic sectors grow or decrease simultaneously are quite rare. The concept of sector rotation is useful to identify, on the one hand, the stage of maturity of the current primary trend and on the other to select those sectors that have a growing relative strength. For example, sectors sensitive to changes in interest rates tend to anticipate both the minimums and the maximums. In contrast, the sectors sensitive to the demand for capital goods or raw materials generally tend to follow the overall trend of the market with delay. Through ETFs, it is possible to take an immediate position on a specific stock, without necessarily being forced to buy the different securities belonging to that particular basket. In this way, it will be possible to obtain immediate exposure to this sector, benefiting at the same time as its growth in value, besides the advantages linked to the diversification.

It is also possible to invest using relative strength, investing, perhaps, on a stock exchange index while benefiting from its growth in value and the advantages linked to diversification.

For example, if one thinks that the US market should grow in relative terms at a given moment to a greater extent than the French one, it will be appropriate to make the first one and underweight the second one. This decision can be reached by analyzing the relative comparative strength between the two markets, which compares two dimensions (composed of market, sector, securities, or other indices) to show how these values are performing comparably. Respect for each other. The trend changes expressed by relative strength generally tend to anticipate the actual ones of the financial activity to which it refers. Therefore, it is possible to use the relative strength to direct purchases towards ETFs that show a growing relative force.

ETFs' high flexibility also allows the construction of guaranteed capital investment; in times of financial turbulence, investors often turn to products that provide capital protection: those provided by financial intermediaries often have high charges for customers. Not many people know that it is possible to build a guaranteed capital product by yourself, which respects your personal investment needs! The central point of the logic of guaranteed capital is interest rates and the duration of the investment. At the base of all, there are two central concepts of finance:

the higher the interest rates, the greater the return on the money as the duration increases, you earn more, because money "works" longer

The money we will obtain in many years can be brought to today, as for bills that follow the discount law (the technical term of bringing the future money to today). You can quickly answer the question: "to have 100 $ in seven years, knowing that the rates are at 5%, how much money do I have to invest?" This statement indicates how much money is needed to invest today to get the desired amount at maturity. The bonds that allow only the fruits to maturity, without paying interest during their life, are called zero-coupon bonds (zcb) and are quite common on the market. If for example, I want to have $ 100 at maturity and interest rates are at 5% I will have to invest in zero-coupon bonds $ 95.24 (if the deadline is between 1 year) $ 78.35 (if the deadline is in 5 years) $ 61.39 (if the deadline is ten years) 48.1 $ (if the deadline is between 15 years) and 23.21 $ (if the deadline is 30 years)

In effect, by building investment with guaranteed capital, one only has to decide how to invest the remaining part of the initial 100 $ that have not been allocated in the zero coupons. An ideal solution could be to invest in options because, thanks to the leverage effect, they can amplify any yield. If you have a less aggressive investment profile, ETFs are excellent tools to build guaranteed capital investment. If, for example, we assume a 10-year investment with rates of 2.5% for that maturity, the portion to be invested in zcb is equal to 78.12%. In comparison, the remaining 21.88% will be invested in the ETF.

This investment strategy makes it possible to achieve a minimum (not real) "money" return target with few operations, as the zcb provides for the repayment only on the nominal amount of the loan (not discounted to the inflation rate). Therefore, it is a valid methodology for those who intend to make investments with clear objectives and have little time to devote to monitoring the values as only an operation until expiry may be necessary. Unlike a guaranteed capital product offered by any financial intermediary, an investment of this kind built independently with ETFs can be dismantled entirely or in pieces (selling only the zcb or existing assets, ETF) to meet any need. Naturally, only at maturity will there be a certainty of the pre-established return and, throughout the loan, a temporary adverse trend in financial variables, (rates rise by lowering the zcb and at the same time decreasing the value of the ETF) could result in the liquidation of losing positions. The same consequence would be selling a structured bond, with the advantage that "doing it at home" the commissions are much lower. You can separate the two components and, if necessary, liquidate only one, according to specific needs.

The profitability of equity (Roe): this is the ratio between the net result and the net assets of a given company. Mainly from equity investments is an essential parameter as profitability higher than the cost of capital is an index of the ability of an enterprise to create value. Therefore, it should be a guarantee of a higher capacity for growth of the securities in the phases of the rise of the market and resistance in the reflexive phases. From this point of view, the Roe is always held in strong consideration by those who choose to invest in shares today.

Price/earnings ratio: a low ratio of this parameter makes a share price particularly attractive, but at the same time, it could mean that expectations regarding future profits are not particularly positive. As in the case of the Roe, this is a factor to be taken into due consideration when choosing the best actions to invest in.

Price-book value ratio: the ratio between the share price and the net asset value resulting from the last balance sheet, especially if this ratio is lower than the unit, means that the company is being paid less than the value of the net budget liabilities. However, this does not necessarily mean that it is a good deal, since the company may not be able to produce profits.

Dividend yield: this is the percentage ratio between the last distributed dividend and the share price, in particular, it measures the remuneration provided by the company to shareholders in the last year in the form of liquidity. This parameter is often taken into account to identify the securities to invest in, since a company able to distribute dividends is generally a good company, but also in this case, as with all the other selection parameters, it is necessary to a broader and more complete analysis since a high level of this indicator could also mean that the company has made few investments or has little prospect of growth. For this reason, looking at the dividend yield as a primary factor in determining the securities to invest in the options market is reductive. The dividend yield only makes sense if accompanied by considerations on any business plans and industrial plans of the listed company. Only in this way is it possible to have guarantees on the prospects of the group.

Chapter 18: How Options Prices are Determined

Alternatives costs are resolved to a limited extent by the cost of the underlying stock.

Be that as it may, alternative costs are also impacted when left to termination and some different elements. We will go over the various ways that the cost of a given alternative can change and what will be behind the changes. It's critical to have a sturdy handle of these ideas, so you don't go into choices as a gullible starting dealer.

The market price of shares

The most significant factor that impacts the cost of an alternative is the cost of the speculation known as the stock that is behind the choice. Be that as it may, it is anything but a 1-1 relationship. The measure of impact from the hidden stock is going to change with time. Moreover, it relies upon whether the alternative is in cash, at the cash, or out of the cash. The portion of the value of the alternative that is because of the cost of the underlying stock is known as the estimation of the appropriate choice.

If an alternative can be equivalent to the market evaluating or not be relatively preferred, it has zero intrinsic worth. A choice would need to be evaluated in cash to have any inherent worth.

✓ For a call choice, if the market cost is lower than the strike cost or the equivalent, the choice will have no estimating at all from the inherent worth. On the off chance that the offer cost is higher than the value used to exchange shares employing the alternative, the choice will have inherent worth.

✓ For a put alternative, if the offer cost is at or over the strike value, the choice will have zero intrinsic worth. If the offer cost is beneath the strike value, at that point, the alternative will have some incentive from the stock. This is called intrinsic worth.

In any case, to confound matters, in any event, when an alternative is at or out of the cash, the cost of the hidden stock has some impact that can change the estimation of choice. The measure of the impact that the market cost of the thing known as the stock has on the cost of the alternative is given by an amount that is called delta. You can peruse the incentive for delta by taking a gander at the information for any choice that you are keen on exchanging. It is a decimal worth running from 0 to 1 for call choices, and it's given as a negative incentive for put choices. The explanation it's given as a negative incentive for put choices is this mirror the way that if the stock cost is found to expand, the cost of a put choice will be diminished. Conversely, if the stock cost decreases, the estimation of the put alternative will increment. It's an inverse relationship, and along these lines, the delta is negative for put choices.

To see how this will play out, how about we take a gander at a particular model. Assume that we have a $100 choice. That is, the strike cost is set to $100. If the cost of the underlying stock is $105, delta for the call choice is 0.77.

That implies that if the dollar estimates the stock increments by $1, the estimation of choice will ascend by around 77 pennies. This is for every offer value change. In this way, for the choice that you are exchanging, there are 100 fundamental offers. Along these lines, a 77-penny cost rise would build the estimation of the alternative by $77.

For a put choice with a similar strike value, the choice would be out of the cash, because they offer cost is higher than the strike cost. For this situation, for the put choice, the delta is given as - 0.23. That implies that the put choice would lose roughly $23 if the offer cost went up by $1. If the offer cost dropped by $1, the put choice would pick up $23.

The inborn estimation of the call alternative portrayed in this hypothetical exercise would be $5 per share. The total expense of choice would be $6.06 per share, mirroring the way that the call choice has $1.06 in extraneous worth. Conversely, the put choice has zero inherent worth. It has nearly the equivalent outward worth, be that as it may, at $1.03.

I have utilized 45 days before lapsing for this activity. Numerical recipes administer alternatives costs, so it's conceivable to make assessments of what the choice cost will be early. There are many numbers of crunchers and spreadsheets that are accessible free online for this reason.

Presently, suppose that instead, the offer cost was $95, with the goal that the get choice was out of the cash, and the put alternative was in cash. For this situation, the call alternative has zero intrinsic worth, and it has a $0.94 outward worth with the goal that the choice would be worth $94. Delta has exchanged, yet not actually. For this situation, for the call choice, the delta is 0.25.

On the off chance that the offer value rose to $96, with

everything else unaltered, the cost of the call alternative would ascend to $1.21 per share. This represents you can even now acquire benefits from less expensive out of the cash choices.

If the offer cost remained at $95, the put choice would have a delta of - 0.75. Notice that if we take the total worth and include the delta for the call and the put alternative, they summarize to 1.0.

In this way, on the off chance that you see a choice of the cell type with a strike that is lower than the market cost, with a delta given by state 0.8, that implies the put alternative with a similar strike cost. The termination date will have a delta of - 0.20.

Delta accomplishes more than give you the expectation of changes in the essential offer cost and value developments of the alternative. Likewise, it gives you a (harsh) gauge of the likelihood to terminate in cash for the agreement known as a choice.

On the off chance that you offer to open, you don't need the alternative to lapse in cash. Subsequently, you are most likely going to sell alternatives that have a little delta. If you purchase to open, you need the alternative to go in the cash, on the off chance that it isn't now. In this way, you would purchase an alternative with a higher delta.

If we state that a given call choice has a delta of 0.66, this shows on the off chance that we see changes to such an extent that the fundamental stock value ascends by $1, the cost of the choice on a for each offer premise will ascend by $0.66. In any case, it likewise reveals to us that there is a 66% possibility that this choice will terminate in a favorable condition: it will be in cash.

Something different you have to know is that delta is dynamic. If the cost of offer increments available, delta ascends for the call alternative and gets littler in size for the put choice. A declining share cost will have the contrary impact.

The sum that delta will change is given by another "Greek" – gamma. Most starting dealers presumably won't be too stressed over gamma; what we've depicted so far is, in reality, all you have to know to go into fruitful alternatives exchanges. In any case, gamma will reveal the variety in the estimation of the delta with an adjustment in stock cost. Thus, if gamma is 0.03, this implies a $1 ascend in the stock cost will build delta by 0.03 for a call choice. The reverse relationship holds for a put choice.

If a choice is at the cash, the delta will be about 0.50 for a call choice and - 0.50 for a put alternative. That bodes well if the strike cost is equivalent to the offer cost available. There is a half likelihood that the market cost will move beneath the strike cost, and there is a half likelihood that the market cost of offers will move over the strike cost.

Implied Volatility

One of the most significant attributes of choices in the wake of considering delta and time rot is the sum a stock cost changes with time. Instability will give you a thought of in what capacity will the value swings of stock are. On the off chance that you take a gander at a stock graph, I am confident that you are accustomed to seeing the cost go all over a great deal, giving a to a great extent sharp bend. The more that it varies, and the greater the vacillations in value, the higher the unpredictability. Everything is relative. Thus, you can't state that any stock has a "flat out" level of unpredictability. What is done is the unpredictability for the whole market is determined. Afterward, the instability of a stock is contrasted with the instability of the market all in all. When taking a gander at the stocks themselves, this is given by an amount called beta.

If the stock, for the most part, moves with the financial exchange everywhere, beta is sure. The off chance that beta is 1.0 implies that it has a similar instability as the whole market. That is a stock with normal unpredictability.

If beta is under 1.0, at that point, the stock doesn't have a lot of instability. The sum beneath 1.0 discloses to you how considerably less unpredictable the stock is in contrast with the market in general. Along these lines, if the beta is given as 0.7, it implies the stock is 30% less unpredictable than the typical market.

On the off chance that beta is more prominent than 1.0, at that point, the stock is more unstable than the normal. If you see a stock with a beta of 1.42, that implies the stock is 42% more unstable than the normal for the market.

Move against the market. At the point when the market goes up, it goes down and the other way around. Most stocks don't have a negative beta. However, they are not hard to track down either.

Instability is a robust amount. When you find it, you are taking a gander at a preview of the unpredictability at that given second. Obviously, under most conditions, it's not liable to change, particularly over brief timeframe periods like half a month or a month. There are exceptional cases to this, including profit season.

Suggested instability is an amount that is given for choices. Suggested instability is a proportion of the certain unpredictability that the stock cost is required to see over the lifetime of choice (that is until the lapse date).

Chapter 19: Importance's of Options Trading

In this chapter, we will outline a few of the primary benefits of trading in options and why you may consider purchasing or offering options as a part of your total trading method. We will also discuss the significant dangers in buying and providing options, remembering that the threats included in options are substantially various for buyers of options compared with the risks for sellers of options.

Benefits of option trading

When purchasing options, you invest in an asset with no real worth, with a minimal life, and which may be worthless within a few months. As you will quickly find, there are numerous benefits of trading options that can be used in a wide variety of methods.

We will now describe a few of the main advantages of options. These are extended attributes that apply to options. As we talk about the types of options in more detail and the methods that can be used for each kind of option, you will see the benefits (and drawbacks) of trading options.

It is likewise fascinating to keep in mind that a benefit to a seller will typically equate as a downside to the buyer and vice versa. The factor this operates in the marketplace is that the seller's reason or strategy is different from the idea the purchaser has participated in the agreement.

Tips

When evaluating the benefits of using options, you likewise need to consider the risks associated with your particular options method.

The benefits we will talk about are:

- Danger management

- Speculation

- Leverage

- Diversification

- Income Generation.

Danger Management

Options provide financiers with the ability to manage danger within their portfolio. Options can provide a financier with a hedge versus falls in the price of their present stock holdings. It can effectively allow a financier to lock in some profits on their holding without physically selling their shares.

This can be useful when an investor wishes to maintain their shares for a longer-term or does not want to understand a capital gain by offering their investment at the current time.

Purchasing a put option allows you to buy the right to sell your present shares at an advantageous price if you anticipate a fall in the cost of those shares before the expiry date of the option. The investors are allowed to gain on the put options that will offset a loss on the physical shares, on the occasion that the stocks do fall in value.

You own 3000 shares in a stock presently trading at $10.50. You want to secure some revenue at this price as you feel that the price is most likely to fall in the brief term. To use this strategy, you purchase 30 put option agreements with a strike cost of $10.50. This costs you to buy $0.20 per share contained in each agreement (with 100 shares in each transaction).

This purchase lets you offer 3000 shares at $10.50 whenever before the options expiry date. Your put option value will increase by a similar quantity (less any ended time worth) if the stock rate subsequently falls. Thus, you are safeguarding yourself against a fall in the price of your stock. A fall in worth of your stock will be balanced by a rise in your options' value.

If the stock cost stays at or above $10.50, then you would either not exercise your options or sell your option close to the expiration date (although it would deserve very little).

If the stock rate does fall to, state, $9.50, then the worth of your put options would increase by $1.00 (less any expired time worth). You could then offer these options for approximately $1.00 and realize earnings of $3000.00. This will balance out the fall in worth of your shareholding of a similar amount. Effectively, you have paid $600.00 for your options to Defend you against the fall in the price of stock position.

Speculation

The capability to trade online and the listing of options on the ASX make it very simple to purchase and offer options. The options trading makes it possible for traders at ease to buy an option contract with the intent of selling the options before the expiration date for a revenue. The traders may have expectations of an increase in the rate of the option (due to a change in the cost of the underlying security). And no objective of ever exercising the option if your option has intrinsic value, the value of your options will change much in line with the change in worth of the underlying stock. You will also see a fall in quality that is unrelated to any change in worth of the hidden security but is due to a fall in the time value of the option as it nears expiry.

How options move with changes in the value of the underlying stock? These movements are for options that have an intrinsic worth in their premium.

As a speculator, you can acquire call options if you expect the rate of the underlying security to increase. As the underlying price of the security rises, your options' intrinsic value will increase by a similar amount if you are anticipating the rate of the underlying security to fall. Your method may be to buy put options as the price of the underlying security drops. The intrinsic options' value will increase by a similar amount. To produce a profit, you need the worth of the underlying security to move in your favor before the expiry date. You would need to offer your option on or before the expiration date.

When purchasing and after offering American style stock options as a method to generate short-term revenue, you need to ensure you sell your options before the expiry date. This requires the cost of the underlying stock to move in your favor before the expiry date.

Leverage
Leverage is the ability to produce the same level of return from a prospective financial investment; however, utilizing a smaller sized initial expense. If you owned the real shares, purchasing a call option with intrinsic value exposes you to a comparable gain or loss that you would attain. The cost of a fraction of the price options of the underlying stock. This permits you to benefit from changes in the stock value without paying the full fee of the capital.

Leverage does come with a new threat; the gains are amplified through the usage, so too are any losses. Some examples show how force can create a more significant portion return than can direct financial investment.

Your returned percentage can be magnified as a result of the leverage achieved through the usage of options. It is necessary to note that your losses can be equally magnified in some circumstances. Nevertheless, your loss will always be limited to the premium you spent on the opportunity when purchasing options.

Idea

When speculating using options, you need to represent the fall in time worth of your option and your deal costs when assessing your trading opportunity.

Diversification

The use of options can offer you the opportunity to benefit from the motion in the stock rate at a portion of the stock price. This permits you to construct a varied portfolio for a lower preliminary expense. This comes at a cost as your options include a value for the time of expiry, which will decrease to no over the option's life.

Income generation

When selling an option, you get an advance premium from the purchaser of your option. The premium kept, whether or not the option has worked out. This premium can produce an income stream if carefully selected options are sold on a systematic basis. The seller maintains the premium and has no further commitment if the options are not exercised.

There are several methods based on offering options to generate premium income. The goal is to sell options that are not likely to be worked out, or purchase back (closeout) your options before the expiration date if there is a danger they will be exercised.

Chapter 20: Advantages and Disadvantages of Option Trading

Advantage

Although options trading began a long term ago, it has a considerable reputation as a risky investment that only experts can understand.

However, for individual investors, options trading can be useful in various aspects. In this section, I will expound on the key advantages options offered and how valuable it is to add it to your portfolio.

Recently, options trading has received full recognition. At the same time, many investors try to stay away from it because they believe it is sophisticated and hard to understand.

Others, who have given it a try, have had a bad experience because of their poor trading background. This situation has led to significant problems with many discouraging others from taking part in trading.

Furthermore, terms like "dangerous" or "risky" has been attached incorrectly to options trading by various financial media and public figures in the financial market.

Notwithstanding, it is vital for investors not to conclude based on this bad experience without getting the other side of the story. This will be impartial and inappropriate to conclude that options trading is risky and dangerous suddenly.

In this book, you will understand four key advantages you will benefit as an investor trading options. With these advantages, you will understand why many people have considered it risky and dangerous.

Cost Efficiency

Trading options gives you significant leverage. Because of this, an investor can get an option position similar to a stock position but offers a better cost-saving opportunity. For instance, you buy 100 shares of a $40 stock, which must result in a payout of $4,000. Nevertheless, if the investor decides to buy two $10 calls (remember each contract is equivalent to 100 shares), the total cost will be $2,000 (2 contracts x 100 shares x $10). The $10 is the market price. From this, the investor has an additional $2,000 to use for whatever purpose.

Although it is not as easy as you see it because the investor must select the right call to buy to make such profit.

For clarity, let us use another example. Assuming you want to buy Apple's share because you anticipate it will rise within several months. So, you bought 150 shares of Apple while trading at $120; the total cost would be $18,000.

Rather than spending so much more, you would decide to select the option imitating the stock closely and purchase the August call option with a predetermined price of $60, for $16. To get a position the same as the 150 shares aforementioned, you have to buy two contracts. This will bring your investment to $32,000 (2 contracts x 100 shares x 16 current market price), which opposes the $18,000 you could have invested.

Less Risky

In Options Trading, you will find situations where buying the options is riskier than you owning equities. Nevertheless, sometimes, you will find when options can help you reduce your risk.

However, this depends on how you choose to use them.

Options trading is less risky for traders because they don't require much financial commitment compared to equities.

Options are safer than stocks because they are the most reliable aspect of hedging. If an investor buys the stock, he has to place a stop-loss order regularly to protect this position.

The purpose of putting the stop order is to stop losses when it reaches its predetermined price set by the investor. Since this looks good, the issue is that it depends on the nature of the order.

For instance, you decide to buy a stock at $150 but don't want to lose anything below 15% of your investment.

So, you decide to place a stop order at $145. This order will be activated once the order sells at or below $145. Peradventure, you woke up the next morning after seeing the stock closed at $151 the previous day and heard that the company's CEO wasn't truthful concerning the earning reports.

Furthermore, there were rumors of embezzlement in the company with the expectation that the stock will open around $120. Once this happens, $120 will be your first trade below the stop order you placed at $145. Immediately, the stock opens, it will first sell at $120. The stop-loss order you activated wasn't there to "save" your investment when you need it.

Peradventure, you trigger the put option to protect your investment, it couldn't have affected you. Options are different in the sense that they don't shut down even when the market closes.

They provide insurance every day of the week. Stop orders cannot do this for you. This is the reason why options are a more positive aspect of hedging.

Additionally, instead of buying the stock, you could have used the stock replacement strategy, which allows you to buy an in the money call option rather than buying the stock.

With individual stock options, you can mimic an equivalent of 75% of the stock performance; however, this cost one-quarter of the stock price.

If you had bought the $145 predetermined price call rather than the stock, your loss would have been limited to the amount you spent. If the option cost you only $6, your loss would have been only $6 rather than the $31.

Higher Profitability

There is no need to use a calculator to determine if you are making the same profit as you are losing money because options trading comes with higher returns.

The example below will clarify that.

Using our previous example, we will comprehend the percentage returns when you bought the stock at $50 and $6, respectively.

Let's assume the option has a delta of 70. This means the price of the option will change 70% of the stock's price change.

Peradventure, the stock rose to $5; your stock's position would return a 10% increase.

Strategic Alternatives

The last benefit to Options trading is the alternative investment opportunity it offers. Options Trading offers a flexible tool and allows investors to recreate their options in many ways.

These positions are called synthetics and offer investors with different means of achieving the same investment goals for their trading.

Even though synthetic positions are regarded as advanced in options trading, they offer various strategic alternatives for investors.

For instance, most investors use brokers who charge a margin when they decide to short a stock. However, some investor doesn't use brokers that offer a margin.

Using options in your trading as an investor allows you to trade the "three dimensions" of the market.

The Bottom Line

From the advantages below, you can agree that those who say Options trading is risky and dangerous are only one-sided.

The opportunity in options trading is limitless, mainly if you undertake to time to understand every aspect of option.

Options trading signify the dawn of a new era for anyone looking to diversify their business or investment. Don't be left behind when you can be at the forefront.

Disadvantages

You may be thinking, are there any disadvantages to options trading? Well, anyone who tells you no is only deceiving you.

Options trading is a short-term investment, and there are bound to be some disadvantages. For instance, if you mistakenly make a wrong prediction on a particular trade, within the next couple of months, you will lose money instead of waiting for years.

Another disadvantage is taxes. You think because you trade online, you won't pay tax. You got that wrong because everything you do on the Options trading market requires you to pay tax.

However, in certain rare cases, you may not pay. Therefore, include that in our business plan and ensure to fill your IRA form before you start investing.

Additionally, you won't have any certificate of deposit when you trade options, unlike shares. The only thing you get when trading options is your paid rights, and this doesn't prove ownership of the option.

Besides this, the issue of uncertainty is a turnoff for most investors. It is scary to invest in something you do not know about. Because of this, most investors take the time to understand everything about the market and investing. With that knowledge, they can quickly turn a loss into a profit. The important thing is to know the strategy you want to use. Endeavor to start small; take only trade you can afford to lose. Options' trading is like learning how to drive.

At first, everything looks scary and impossible. However, with time behind the wheel, you begin to perfect your driving skills. Over time, you start using a single hand to turn the steering; options trading works similarly. To be at the top, you have to practice, learn, and unlearn what you have learned.

Conclusion:

At every level of options trading, there are mistakes that people do over and over again. However, these mistakes must be avoided to realize a profit from the trade.

If you ever hope to make money in trading options successfully, then there are several skills that you will want to hone as much as possible, starting with the ability to trade like a robot. When you have a trade on the line that could make or break you, it is only natural to be scared or anxious. Still, those emotions are only going to cloud your judgment if left unchecked, which is why it so essential to box them up and bury them in the ground when you are trading so you can only focus on the facts in front of you. Fail to do so, and you will watch in fear as your sure thing turns into a considerable loss instead of jumping into action right away to salvage as much profit as possible.

Being a successful trader means being able to react at a moment's notice, without hesitation, full stop. The only way you can ever ensure that this is going to be the case is if you can put aside the emotional aspect of what is occurring and focus on the numbers as if it were others' money. An excellent way to ensure that this is possible is to make it a point of never putting more on the line then you can afford to lose.

Having come to the end of this guide, it is natural to have confidence in yourself and your ability to trade successfully. This is no reason to get ahead of yourself, however, which means having measured expectations when it comes to your success when you are first starting out. Don't forget, options trading is one of the more difficult types of investment trading to do successfully, even for those who have been at it for years which means you are likely in for an uphill battle before you start seeing any sort of reliable results for all the effort you are going to need to put in from the start.

As such, if you expect too much too soon, all you will end up doing is hurting your confidence and making it more difficult for you to get back on the horse after you have been knocked off. Instead, it is best to keep in mind that trading successfully is a skill which means that the only way to improve is with plenty of good old fashioned practice. Remember, successfully trading options is a marathon, not a sprint, slow and steady wins the race.

If you enjoyed reading this book, please let me know your thoughts by leaving a short review on Amazon. It means a lot to me. Thank you.